Thoughtful Caregiving

Abuse Prevention Through Emotional Responsibility

Matthew Starr

KeyLight Press, LLC
Mt. Vernon, OH

Dear Uncle Mark
& Aunt Becky,

Courage and
 inner peace!

Love,
 Matt :)

Copyright © 2010 by Matthew Starr

All rights reserved. No part of this publication may be reproduced, stored or transmitted in any form, without the prior written permission from the copyright owner and publisher. The text, layout and designs presented in this book, as well as the book in its entirety, are protected by the copyright laws of the United States (17 U.S.C. 101 et seq.) and similar laws in other countries.

All case details and client information, though based on real cases, people and events, have been changed to protect clients' confidentiality rights.

Thoughtful Caregiving is published by
KeyLight Press, LLC,
Mount Vernon, OH.

Cover photo [2009] Lisa F. Young. Image from Bigstock.com

Book editing and design by Black Cat Creative Services, Cleveland, OH

Library of Congress Cataloging-in-Publication Data
Starr, Matthew
Thoughtful caregiving: abuse prevention through emotional responsibility
1. Caregiving   2. Abuse prevention   3. Emotional responsibility

ISBN: 9780615294957

Contents

Acknowledgements 5

Foreword 8

Introduction—People Are Getting Hurt! 11

Chapter 1: Your Life As A Consumer 14

Chapter 2: Abuse Prevention 21

Chapter 3: The Trouble With Emotions 28

Chapter 4: One Day A Provider, the Next A Consumer 37

Chapter 5: The Impact of Emotions 58

Chapter 6: Code of Silence 66

Chapter 7: My Brother's Keeper 73

Chapter 8: A Call To Courage 86

Chapter 9: Why Are People Still Getting Hurt? 92

Chapter 10: Anti-Caregiving Terrorism 98

Chapter 11: Which Way Forward? 120

Acknowledgements

You never know how and when you have an influence on people. I have always felt that no matter where you are, someone is watching you, seeing how you conduct yourself, treat the world, and make decisions. With that in mind, there are several people who I need to thank in encouraging me to write this book.

I consider Arlene MacNamara to be a close friend. Her vigilance and encouragement to keep Roger's work alive has been tremendously supportive to me. We continue to share stories we hear, read about, and experience first-hand about abuse and neglect cases. She understands that abuse continues to challenge our society, and her hopefulness keeps this subject matter burning brightly.

My business partner and co-producer from I-CONN Video Production, Nancy Lorey, also helped me follow through on this book. Nancy met Roger before I did, but it was after a seminar where the two of us talked with him about producing some training videos. Nancy's organizational skills and her understanding from a learner's eyes continue to make me think before I pick up pen and paper. We saw some pretty remarkable scenarios as we set out filming the series from Connecticut, Montana, and Ohio—all caregiving settings that Roger had strongly influenced.

My parents, Glenn and Linda, also were happy that I pursued this book. Dad, in particular was pleased because of his help filming Roger in Connecticut for the DVD series. Dad was so taken with Roger, as was Roger with my dad, that Roger frequently called him his "fierce warrior."

My wife Joanne continues to support and tolerate my entrepreneurial lifestyle and associated activities, which includes writing this book. Additionally, she understands my zest for living and what gives me inner peace whether it's making movies, acting, singing, running an advertising agency, hunting, or anything else that may tickle my muse.

I would be remiss in not thanking one of my first supervisors, Martha Richardson, who was extremely helpful and supportive to me when I reported my first case of abuse back in the 1990s. All caregivers would be fortunate to have a Martha in their lives. She continues to serve as a noble professional in caregiving, and I'm proud to have served with her.

Glenn Bryan is another very good friend of mine whose opinion, experience, insight, and own career I value greatly. His sincere and genuine concern for others is an example for all of us. Many of my ideas for this book and other projects emerged from Glenn and I visiting over coffee and debating, discussing, and dissecting ideas and concepts that we'd like to see change the world. We continue to meet for coffee and stimulating conversation to which I always look forward.

A very special thank you goes to Janna Miller who did an excellent job of choosing her mom and dad. You continue to inspire me. To Janna's parents, Rick and Barb, thank you for being champions and my friends. You're the best.

My editor and friend, Randy Wood of Black Cat Creative Services in Cleveland, is probably one of the great readers of my generation. His intelligence and sharp wit with a genuine love for good writing, has challenged and encouraged me with each draft of this book. We've crossed paths three times, first when I was in college, again during graduate school, then we reconnected again, twenty-years later, when I discovered he is a book editor. Without missing a beat, we picked up conversations with each other from long ago. Randy also was my mentor and supervisor when I was a resident assistant as an undergraduate. He was beside me when I had to bust my friends and football teammates for breaking campus policy. I will always remember the courage and support he showed with me during those unpleasant incidents of having to investigate and present disciplinary cases against my friends. Most of my friends and teammates understood and accepted the fact that I was in a role of leadership and conviction that I took an oath to enforce my school's policies for conduct. However, it was a challenge when some of these same people were supposed to have your back on the football field. It was rough, but Randy's example, mentoring, and friendship made the difference. Who knew that I would experience similar cases with more dire stakes in my future career?

Finally, Roger, my captain, I miss you and look forward to seeing you again.

Foreword

In 1975, Roger MacNamara was named chief administrator of a large, caregiving organization legally mandated to serve more than two-thousand people spread across various residences, including a central institution, nursing homes, supervised apartments, group residences and in their own homes. This administrative spectrum was a true continuum of responsibility. After ten years at this institution, he resigned to write, travel, and consult. He was in the habit of keeping notes in a journal and wrote many articles for various publications. Given the breadth of his experience and events that occurred during those years, he contemplated writing a book about human services from the vantage point of his former position. However, he was not certain of the theme for a book about his service to handicapped and elderly persons.

At dinner one evening with a close friend, he discussed his intention to write a book and his difficulty with finding the theme. His friend asked Roger what his most vivid recollection was of the beginning of his tenure. Roger remembered immediately. On his second day, the state's chief negotiator called to inform him of a disciplinary hearing in progress at the state capitol and that his presence was required. It would have to be Roger's decision to accept or reject any negotiated agreement. In preparation for his appearance the next morning, Roger called his personnel director to his office and asked him to recount the charges against the employees who were terminated. He offered a few examples: slapping, tripping, kicking, force-feeding one individual a lighted cigarette, and encouraging a sexually aroused man to expose his genitals to other residents. Roger's friend responded that that was the book he should write, and to write it from his experience. And he did.

Roger realized that he had covered only half of the story and immediately began writing his next book. One afternoon, sometime after the second book was published, we were discussing what the next step should be. The books were just the beginning of Roger's vision for helping vulnerable children and adults in caregiving facilities. He excused himself and went upstairs to his office. A couple of hours later he emerged with the first issue of The Abuse Prevention Monitor, a monthly newsletter dedicated to calling attention to abuse and its prevention. Roger also wrote manuals containing abuse-prevention principles and techniques.

Subscribers to the newsletter requested that he present training seminars, which he did all over the country. At one of those seminars, a gentleman approached him – Matt Starr.

To quote Matt, "I first met Roger at a seminar held at the facility where I was working full time. He stood about 6'2" so we could look each other in the eyes. You knew this guy was listening to you when you spoke. His presence immediately brightened the dimly lit conference room where we held much of our training."

"On this day in 1999, he began talking about how abuse and neglect were rooted more in organizational problems and less of an instance where a bad person was harming someone else. For me, it was pretty radical to hear such rhetoric, and I could tell by the reaction of most seminar participants that they were unsettled by the whole principle of abuse being built into the organization. I liked him immediately."

"Roger would have been a good lawyer because he was very adept at getting to the truth of the matter. He often asked questions of his protégés to which he already knew the answers. At the same time, he challenged you to dissect these abuse cases and get at the heart of the sad and unfortunate instances. This conversation and others like it were the basis of the video series we produced."

"He continued to preach that abuse doesn't just happen. We fail to see the signs leading to the act. Roger said more than once that he really didn't like to talk about abuse because it's the sense of conflict which is what is central to abuse happening in the first place. A home, work setting, or day program without conflict is likely to be free from abuse."

Matt understood and embraced the essence of Roger's approach to abuse prevention and the principles to put it into practice right from his introduction to it.

Roger was working on his third book when he passed away. I like to think that Matt, without ever seeing Roger's notes, has finished the book for him.

Arlene Mirsky-MacNamara

Introduction—People Are Getting Hurt!

Caregiving is a daunting task which exacts a heavy emotional, physical and financial toll.

—Tommy Thompson, former HHS Secretary and Governor of Wisconsin

Abuse doesn't just happen. It builds up and we fail to see the signs. When we know what causes abuse, then we can prevent it. Our hope is that readers will take the opportunity to review the forthcoming materials, think about the discussion questions, and take a critical look at their own ways of managing care delivery.

This book is based on Roger MacNamara's work, which continues through his company, www.FreedomFromAbuse.org. Several of Roger's publications and videos are located at that site. We aim to continue Roger's work to prevent abuse in caregiving settings.

It's important for readers to understand a little about the man who started all of this. If there ever was a person in the history of human services who devoted his life to preventing abuse, Roger Dale MacNamara is that person. Roger had been a college instructor, a teacher, a consultant, a career service provider and administrator but, most of all, a friend and mentor to many in human services.

Throughout his career, Roger was instrumental in forging monumental changes in human services, including institutional reform in the 1960s, institutional litigation in the 1970s, establishing state-private partnerships in the 1980s, and increasing privatization and entrepreneurial initiatives in the 1990s. He was the founder of

Abuse Prevention Specialists™, and author of *Freedom from Abuse* (1988), and *Creating Abuse-free Caregiving Environments for Children, the Disabled, and the Elderly* (1992). Roger also contributed a number of articles to professional and lay journals and periodicals.

Roger was honored by the Connecticut Chapter of the American Association of Mental Retardation as Professional of the Year and was recognized by act of the Connecticut Legislature for Meritorious Service. He served on the Connecticut State Developmental Disabilities Council and was a member of the Connecticut Task Force on Autism.

Roger's academic achievements, professional accomplishments, and the honors bestowed upon him can only suggest the vitality, passion and compassion of his leadership. To know Roger was inspirational and life-changing. These are only a few of the reasons we must continue his work.

Roger was my friend, and I continue to converse with his wife, Arlene, who is just as committed to abuse prevention as he was. The core of his mission was teaching caregivers to be emotionally responsible for the care and well-being of the consumers who entrust them to support their daily needs. To that end, Roger developed the 18-point Caregiver's Oath which follows, as an effective means to help healthcare professionals keep their compassionate duty toward others top-of-mind as they work with people in need.

The Caregiver's Oath

Does this fit easily into your company policy and training manuals?

1. I shall abide by state laws and agency policies regarding humane treatment of persons for whom I am responsible.
2. I shall defend clients'/consumers' right to proper, safe, comfortable and dignified care.
3. I understand that all forms of corporal punishment are prohibited.

Thoughtful Caregiving

4. I understand that all forms of demeaning, insulting, threatening language or gestures are prohibited.
5. I shall refrain from all forms of rough handling, excessively forceful or unauthorized interventions.
6. I shall not engage in emotional or sexual harassment or approach, manipulate or coerce clients/consumers into sexual activities or discussions.
7. I understand that there is no circumstance that shall warrant the use of harmful force.
8. I understand that I am accountable for the judgment I use in determining what shall or not cause a client/consumer harm as a result of my actions or inaction.
9. I shall refrain from the use of obscene, profane or offensive language in my role as caregiver.
10. I shall not add to a client's/consumer's distress by my response.
11. I shall avoid needless confrontations.
12. I shall employ interventions only after I have attempted less intrusive means of distracting or calming a client/consumer.
13. I shall never retaliate against a consumer for his or her actions against me, a co-worker, or another client/consumer.
14. I shall prevent harm by separating aggressive persons or removing clients/consumers who might be endangered by them.
15. I shall call for assistance whenever I feel a client/consumer is becoming agitated or might be calmed by the presence of another person.
16. I shall report abuse and neglect or actions by co-workers that might result in abuse or neglect.
17. I shall not experiment with methods not duly authorized by the client's/consumer's treatment team.
18. I shall ask for help or additional training when I am confused or concerned about my responses to clients/consumers.

~~Chapter 1~~

Your Life As A Consumer

Do unto others as you would have them do unto you.

—Luke 6:31

Imagine you are in a body without the ability to walk by yourself. You try to talk but cannot get your vocal cords, tongue, mouth, and air to all work together so that you can express your thoughts and feelings. All that you can manage is a groan or scream at limited tones and pitches. You are living in a home for people with "special needs" or "extra needs"—lingo that has become the flavor of the month in your world.

Physically, you cannot do many things for yourself because your shaky hands have lost their fine motor skills. The resulting muscle atrophy has made feeding yourself feel like climbing Mount Everest. Using the bathroom and bathing are another real treat. There is no way you can manage yourself safely in the bathroom which, if left on your own (much as you'd prefer it), is a room full of land mines and trip hazards. Once in awhile, you manage to make some small accomplishment on your own, such as actually making it to the toilet before you urinate, turning on the water faucet to just the right temperature so you can rinse off your face and hands without scalding yourself, and even generating enough power to open the door as you pound the kick plate with the footrest of your wheelchair. During your baths, most of the time, more soap hits the bottom of the floor and tub than your skin and washcloth. You have to lift your arm,

Thoughtful Caregiving

which feels glued to your side due to severe muscle contraction and is painful, when your caregivers attempt to move it in the slightest for you.

Today is special; it is the day your care team is meeting with you to review your annual Program Plan! Your care team has assembled in your kitchen to go over what you need to do over the next year in order for you to enjoy your life. These very knowledgeable professionals discuss everything about you, your accidents over the past year, your progress on last year's goals, your mood swings, even the size and frequency of your bowel movements. Incredulously, you look at the faces of these people (most of them are strangers to you) as they smile and appear to be genuine but you conclude that they have no clue. And those closest to you, your caregivers, remain silent until it is time to talk about the difficulties you have in life that are embarrassing to you. You feel like you've been transported to the Planet of the Apes.

"She spills more food than she puts in her mouth. I can't get her to slow down," your support staff says. "And she can't do anything for herself in the bathroom...."

This litany of complaints drones on as you sit there surrounded by these people, some of whom are the same as last year, while some are new. The new ones glance at you momentarily then immediately look away to the person speaking. If they notice you staring back at them, they offer a brief smile before turning away. You want to say, "Hello, how are you? Who are you? You may have introduced yourself to me months ago when you were hired, but just tell me who the hell you are again—please?" No one asks you any questions.

More people share their assessments of your ability levels and speak in terms above your head. This meeting has become an out-of-body experience that no matter what someone might say or do, you can't quite believe that this is your life now. The people at your kitchen table write down words; your plan solidifies on paper or the laptops that some brought to the meeting. You keep hearing the word, "Medicaid" and wonder what the hell this has to do with your life but, apparently, your goals for the next year are a continuation of the goals you have had for the past 15 years—help you improve your skills in toileting, eating, bathing, brushing what's left of your teeth, and communicating with others. For this goal, your team has given you a communication board that allows you to touch or point to a symbol on this massive, one-volume, voice-activated contraption telling everyone within twenty-five feet that you want a beverage or that you have to use the toilet.

You think to yourself, "Is this what my life has been reduced to? Coffee, pee, and accidents?" Your team then looks at you after everyone else has spoken. Like a scene from the Twilight Zone, the person doing most of the writing finally asks you if you have anything to add. Stunned, you just stare at their faces and say nothing. Inside you're shocked and saddened by what these people have decided for you to do. Still, they await an indication from you during this awkward pause. "What's the point?" you ask yourself. "It doesn't matter that I don't care to work on the goals these people decided for me by order of some obscure Health Department regulation." Your only recourse is to try telepathy.

"Forget the damn communication board unless my voice-activated options are 'I want to run my toes in the sand by the ocean,' or 'No bingo tonight, please. I think I'll stay in and read a book,' or 'Bring me some fresh fruit and veggies instead of the high-fructose-corn-syrup ridden crap you purchased from the low bidder.'"

In addition to the other goals, your team is actively pursuing physical therapy for you to help with your severe muscle contraction, which will hopefully increase your range of motion in your arm and shoulder joints. PT is scheduled twice each week, but it has become an acronym for Pain Tolerance instead of physical therapy. The twice-a-week frequency of your "therapy" is futile unless aggressively pursued and supplemented at least twice daily and then only after a warm bath, when your muscles are loose and relaxed. Occasionally, your caregivers try to get to it, but it offers nothing but throbbing

Thoughtful Caregiving

because they aren't skilled enough in properly administering your range-of-motion activities. As a result, your shoulder and arms are bruised, which is charted and passed off as "chronic bruising".

A week after your plan meeting, you find yourself sitting in your wheelchair in an adult diaper so bulky that your clothing stretches, nearly ripping apart at the seams—you feel like the Stay-Puft Marshmallow Man. "Damn it!" you say to yourself, "Someone put my communication board in with the rest of the activity items (which are nothing more than toys to you that you gave away to your church's charity yard sale when you were ten-years old). I don't know who the hell dressed me this morning, but apparently they didn't get the memo—I don't wear a f———ing diaper!"

Sometimes tears well to the surface, but you've learned to disguise your pain. Having occasionally been discovered sobbing by the people taking care of you as you lament your existence, they sometimes offer a small pat on the hand; some have even offered an occasional hug. Others have seen you, shook their heads, then wrote in your chart titled Behavior Notes, "Found crying for no apparent reason," followed by the date. Beyond those entries that manage to make it into the chart, that is all that is written about you. There are no notes about the time you laughed at someone's joke. There's no record of the time you were so proud of the fact that you drank your entire cup of coffee without spilling a drop. There is nothing mentioned of your dreams to walk again, to meet the love of your life, to write a book, to attend your family reunion, to find someone who will understand you, to have someone around this hell hole leave you alone when you want privacy, or to find something fun for you to do when you want to do it—not according to their schedule. There's nothing in the chart that says, "Followed the schedule today, appeared content," which would be a dubious understatement.

Your mornings begin with an abrupt announcement from your caregiver, "It's time to get up," as she turns on the bedroom lights at 6:30 a.m. No matter how many times this happens, you still cannot get used to the jarring noise and intense, artificial light burst as the person providing your care this day thrusts you into the day. You prefer to awaken slowly, to follow your own circadian rhythm by gradually gliding into the day over a cup of coffee and quiet reflection watching nature's small animals forage outside your window. No, not here; everyone eats breakfast at 7:30 a.m. and you are scheduled for your bath at 6:45 a.m.—no exceptions. One of your caregivers who actually listened to you and let you sleep a little longer, was reprimanded for not being able to get her work done expeditiously. Furthermore, she was ridiculed by her colleagues for not keeping up with them. It was no surprise that this person found employment elsewhere, and you had no say in the matter.

You don't say anything because you don't want to rock the boat or make things harder for the staff. You've learned that it's not pleasant to make others wait on you. Some of the other people living in your home (whom everyone around you calls your "peers," which you cannot fathom—you didn't pick them) have been punished for their resistance and noncompliance to the schedule. You've seen them held down on the cold, hard linoleum to the point of tears and humiliation. Even when the supervisor comes by, her tolerance and acceptance of your caregivers' actions are justified. You ask yourself, "Whose home is this anyway? Am I a patient? An inmate? A resident?" Gradually it hits you. You know what you are and can do nothing about it.

"My God! I am a consumer!" You realize that you consume time, energy, attention, and resources at your "home." "I may as well be cattle on a farm. Consumer? Really? I'm not shopping right now—I don't think so, anyway," you say to yourself when you hear this word. As a consumer you have no option but to share your life with others, others whom someone else has chosen. And in this community, you must wait for other consumers to finish their business with the people providing them with care. Your appointments and time are also limited because other consumers are waiting their turns.

You've been at this home long enough to know which caregivers can be trusted and who can not. You can see it in their eyes. Joe, who is always complaining about management, seeks ways to "stick it to

Thoughtful Caregiving

the man." He's only there to collect a paycheck and to watch television (mostly your television it seems) and he watches only the programs he likes. Darlene is nice but she's meek. She will only do what is expected of her not because she has no initiative, but because she's afraid the other caregivers will give her grief for being too productive or caring. Flo is constantly on her cell phone consoling her daughter who is pregnant again by her deadbeat boyfriend. Flo works a ton of overtime to help pay her grandchildren's bills. This is her third straight day of double shifts. You're extremely cautious because her temperament is like a loose cannon ready to explode any minute. Already, you've seen how irritated she can become when you don't do what she wants you to do. Then there's the staff member at night sitting outside your bedroom "monitoring" everyone and checking on you and your "peers" as he entertains himself with an aromatic French vanilla latte and Nintendo DS™ "smack down" video game while you try to sleep.

Max is your absolute least favorite. He is slick-tongued and says things to his supervisor and other people paid to protect you and your "peers," but he knows the system and thumbs his arrogance in the faces of authority figures managing your home. You've seen him yank people around, laughing at them. He hasn't done it to you because you don't challenge him, but you wonder how long it will be before you end up on his shit list. He's gone through the years unchallenged. After an incident, he was finally investigated for excessive force bordering on physical abuse (turned in by a rookie employee), he lost his job but became a martyr; the rookie resigned. And your life as you knew it was reduced even more because Max appealed and was reinstated to his work area with full back-pay of wages during his absence. Guess who's working in your home tonight?

For too many people receiving care at residential facilities, this is a characteristic snap shot of their lives as consumers. Don't misunderstand, this scenario is not the case for the majority of consumers in many reputable facilities. There are many dedicated, professional, compassionate caregivers working in private homes and residential facilities. This snap shot, though based on real stories and events, is not intended to indict or expose the caregiving profession. It is intended to give readers a view of residential caregiving from the perspective of a care recipient who feels powerless. For many consumers, the care they receive feels inflicted upon them; their dignity and freedom stripped away.

There is a better way for the caregiving profession to approach how we care for our consumers. Reviewing and implementing the standards of *The Caregiver's Oath* is a good place to start. Individuals needing care and assistance from professional caregivers should not feel like they have been institutionalized. In properly managed caregiving facilities, consumers feel like their personal cares are attended to along with their care needs. They see themselves as functioning members of thriving communities. The solution is to train managers, supervisors and direct-care employees to focus on emotionally responsible caregiving. I will discuss this concept more fully in later chapters.

~~Chapter 2~~

Abuse Prevention

Patience and fortitude conquer all things.

—Ralph Waldo Emerson, American poet, 1803–1882

Caregiving in the United States is a multi-billion dollar industry when you consider the number of child day cares, adult/senior care centers and hospital facilities. Facilities are for-profit as well as nonprofit, large and small scale. There are nearly 17,000 nursing home facilities in the U.S. today and the number of residents in them is growing.

Myths and Precursors That Contribute To Abusive Caregiving

Caregiving is the impact point of human services, and whatever management style is in use, from total quality management to traditional line authority, if employee supervision and evaluation are not organized around an explicit set of emotionally responsible caregiving principles, abuse and neglect will continue to be ever-present dangers.

Myths that Maintain or Contribute to Abusive Caregiving:

- "Abuse doesn't happen here. Our employees care."
- "Abuse is a human problem. We punish it, but it happens."
- "I knew something was wrong, but I didn't know what to do. People tell me that if you report, bad things will happen to you."
- "Management does not want to hear about abuse."

- "We felt that he/she was abusive, but we had no proof."
- "We could see that she/he was losing control, but what could we do? Getting the person in trouble wasn't the answer."
- "Our supervisor controls communication."

Are Abuse Precursors Present In The Caregiving Environment?

Are scolding, correcting, and punishing central features of consumer care? Is there immoderate use of "hands" even for support or guidance? Are restraints excessive or avoidable? Are there invisible restraint patterns? Are employees preoccupied with consumer behavior? Do employee reports contain editorial remarks about consumers or employee circumstances? Are employees defensive and cliquish? Is employee language coarse, stylized, or excessively sarcastic? Is there informal specialization within the employee group?

Are employees constantly blaming someone for something? Are complaining parents or relatives dismissed as "unreasonable?" Are problem employees able to evade accountability for poor performance? Do employees act or talk as if they were victims?

Do supervisors know "invisible" forms of abuse? Do supervisors know abuse indicators for consumers and employees? Who sees potentially explosive employees? Deteriorating employees? Are employees amused by the two-levels-of-care game—the one we know and the one we show?

What Do Supervisors, Managers, and Executives Know About Abuse?

In 2000, Eileen Furey and Marikje Keharhan published a study titled, "What Supervisors, Managers, and Executives Should Know About Abuse of People with Mental Retardation" in the *Developmental Disabilities Bulletin* [Vol. 28 (2)]. In their study, Furey and Keharhan discovered that persons occupying key leadership positions in our home-service providers and day programs are not necessarily aware of what causes abuse, the characteristics of people who are likely to be the victims of abuse, the characteristics of potential abusers, and how organizational policies, procedures, and practices can contribute to or prevent abuse and neglect.

Abuse is not planned, rather it is the result of the interaction of stress, frustration, organizational variables, characteristics of the victim and abuser, and the work environment, which, when combined, create an unstable situation resulting in abuse. None of these factors should ever be accepted or interpreted as excuses for abuse and neglect. While every person possesses the capacity to abuse, additional studies suggest there are personal attributes that may increase the likelihood of a person abusing another (Haddock & McQueen, 1983; Luthana & Perlow, 1993; Marchetti & McCartney, 1990; McCartney, 1992; Perlow & Latham, 1993). However, this does not mean that every staff person who internalizes anger and frustration will become an abuser. To put it another way, just as every thunderstorm has the potential to become violent—the interplay of hot and cold winds, air pressure, thunder and lightening—very few actually produce tornadoes. And it takes a schooled and seasoned meteorologist to spot the truly violent storms as they form and to warn those in the storm's path of the danger. In caregiving, a keenly sensitive and emotionally aware supervisor can exercise the critical intervention to recognize the signs in the staff—aggravation, frustration, and dismay—and be a supportive influence in a positive manner before the staff person reaches the point of abuse.

Furey and Keharhan sited previous research (Sundram, 1986) and uncovered a social dilemma in instances where a person was fired from their job for substantiated abuse. They concluded that in these cases, organizations often failed to go through the process of delivering appropriate consequences for the staff member and the organization after substantiating the abuse. "Appropriate consequences" may mean retraining, examining potential organizational factors that may have contributed, altering schedules, providing more supervision, coaching, or support to staff, and termination. Instead, leadership may have allowed the person found responsible for the substantiated abuse to resign. This outcome does not protect the men and women who receive services. First, it absolves the organization from self-examining and taking responsibility for possible organizational factors leading to the abuse. Second, the employee can go to work for another human service agency since he or she doesn't have a record of termination. In both instances, neither the organization or the former employee have addressed the abuse situation.

We see evidence of substantiated abuse in the news constantly. The hours of talk show debates and horrifying images of staff caught on film violently beating the men and women played in slow motion over and over. These images stir volatile emotions inside each of us, and so we demand justice. Sundram, in 1986 mind you, argued that not every abuser should be automatically fired. The extreme cases of abuse highlighted on broadcast news and exposé shows suggest that we terminate the employee with no questions asked. Nowadays, we pursue criminal action on top of that, which in the extreme cases of abuse would appear justified. These instances, however, are not typical abuse cases. There are degrees of abuse, and while "major" and "minor" are the best categories we can muster to describe abuse, not all abuse is equally as serious. The crux of this situation is having only one consequence of substantiated abuse whether minor or major and results in an unnerving effect on the incidents reported.

Reporting a coworker for abuse is one of the hardest things a caregiver can do. Believing that their colleague will lose his or her job if they report, staff generally will not report even minor abuse. The extreme cases of abuse are not, in most cases, the first instance that the caregiver commits the act. Abuse typically begins with inappropriate interactions that escalate to minor abuse, and if it is not corrected early, the employee is likely to repeat it, eventually leading the caregiver's interactions spiraling toward major abuse.

Speaking of automatically firing an employee for substantiated abuse, the organizational leadership may be extremely proud of its decisiveness. The agency leadership may even be praised publicly for having the fortitude to be "tough" in the public eye. However, the organization and its leadership then fail to take the next step, to study their own policies, procedures, organizational culture, and social climate that may have led to the abusive act. While decisive and firm with the employee, the leadership has done nothing more to ensure a safe environment for the men and women in their care.

Roger MacNamara's recommendations in his video, *The Caregiving Personality*, are echoed in the conclusions Furey and Keharhan identified in their study (pp. 58-60):

1. Training:
   - All supervisors, managers, and executives need continuous training in detecting and preventing abuse and neglect including targeted training on characteristics of victims, potential abusers, and substantiated abuse.
   - Give supervisors and managers regular access to the "facts" and outcomes associated with specific abuse reports so they can learn more about the entire process of reporting, investigating, substantiating, resolving, and consequating abuse.
   - Offer specific training for supervisors to assess work climate and culture; brainstorm, select and implement improvements/solutions.
2. Hiring and Probationary Period
   - At the very least, hiring should include police background checks, extensive interviews, full follow-up on letters of recommendation and employment history.
   - Expand hiring practices to include giving potential employees a case to which they must respond, a statement of their personal beliefs about persons with disabilities, and other activities that will provide insight into attitudes toward people they will serve and the field in general.
   - To the extent possible, consumers should be involved in interviewing and hiring employees.
   - Extend the probationary period for new employees to one year.
   - Make full use of the probationary period and the specific evaluation points to cull out those who are not well suited for work in mental

retardation services before they become permanent employees.

3. Agency Response to Reports of Abuse:
   - If firing is the only response to abuse, it will reduce reporting and make it more likely that abuse will occur.
   - Many supervisors have said that employees are hesitant to report because they believe that nothing is being done in response to their reports. Therefore, agencies should make individuals aware of the actions and outcomes associated with each report of abuse within the boundaries of employee confidentiality and rights.
   - Since employees look at the agency's response to determine future actions, it is important that all employees know what to expect when they report abuse.

4. Performance Appraisal and Progressive Discipline
   - Performance appraisal and feedback should be constant. Supervisors must use both day-to-day feedback practices as well as the formal performance appraisal system (annual, semi-annual, quarterly) to recognize and reward positive interactions and skilled work.
   - Agencies should support supervisors to fine-tune their progressive discipline skills in order to more effectively create the necessary paper trail to eliminate employees who are performing below expectations.

5. Policy Implementation
   - Agencies must look more closely at whether the policies and procedures they have written to protect people from abuse can be and are being fully implemented. Agencies should consider convening groups of supervisors to examine the implementation issues around specific policies and procedures and use their input to improve the policy-reality match.

6. Role of Supervisors
   - Supervisors cannot adequately perform their jobs if they are counted in coverage. Management must examine their expectations of supervisors if they are put in coverage and assure that the

important supervisor tasks are being attended to.
- Supervisors are truly the direct link between management and the people who are being served. They must be valued and respected for the skills and knowledge they bring to the day-to-day work of the organization.

With a rapidly growing number of consumers of caregiving services, adopting these abuse-prevention strategies is the key to advancing caregiving into the next phase.

~~Chapter 3~~

The Trouble With Emotions

First keep the peace within yourself, then you also can bring peace to others.

—Thomas à Kempis, German monk, 1380–1471

Trouble In The Checkout Line:

A few weeks ago my wife, Joanne, was standing in a checkout lane at a department store returning some items. She was in the "Return Only" lane (register #1) and was the next person in line. To her far right, another patron just arrived at register #5. She said that she wanted to return some items. The associate asked the customer to go to the register #1 for returns and explained that she was not authorized to handle return transactions. The associate even pointed to the "Return Only" sign adjacent to the turn-style maze for patrons wishing to make purchases.

In a loud, boisterous huff, the patron grabbed her items, said something terrible to the associate at register #5, and then cut right in front of Joanne, nearly shoving her out of the way in order to take care of her returns.

So, my wife said in a calm voice, "Excuse me, the line for returns is right here. I am next." Even the associate at register #1 (the lane exclusively for returns), said that the line jumper needed to wait for her turn.

Thoughtful Caregiving

The woman snapped around at my wife and said, "Oh no! Don't go there with me today! Not today! I was in line, and they didn't tell me that I had to come over here 'til I got all the way up there. I ain't standing in line any more! I ain't waiting. You're just going to have to wait for me!" The associate was embarrassed. Joanne was furious. The woman created a scene that challenged the associates and my wife.

Has this ever happened to you? You've probably grasped that this scenario can teach us about people. What do you suppose happened next? Ask yourself these questions:
- How would you have handled this situation if this happened to you?
- How should the sales associates have handled the situation?
- How does this episode relate to organized caregiving?

I guess I could have also asked, "How would you like to have responded to this person?" That would be different from how do you actually respond to this person, huh?

Okay, so here's what happened. Joanne bit her tongue and let the rude patron go ahead to return her items despite the person's line-jumping and belligerent attitude. Remaining calm and poised on the outside only masked the anger my wife felt inside. This woman challenged and embarrassed my wife in public—at least that's how my wife felt about it.

Once the rude and angry patron left the store, and Joanne reached the checkout counter, the sales associate apologized to Joanne and thanked her for her patience and tolerance. Everyone in the main checkout line was also watching. After returning her items, Joanne left the store and immediately called me to vent.

At first, she felt wronged, unjustly attacked, and weak because she didn't stand up against this rude person. She further explained that she didn't deserve to be treated like that. I concurred and said, "Dear, you did the right thing by letting it go."

Still upset by the situation, we continued talking. "Think about it," I said. "Did you lose your temper?"

"No."

Did you maintain your poise?"

"Yes."

"Would further confrontation be worth it?"

"No."

"Then, you walked away with your dignity in tact. You should celebrate how well you handled the situation. I'm proud of you for maintaining control of your emotions."

Her demeanor changed, and she admitted that what I said made a lot of sense (I wrote that down right away—some days I am good, baby!).

Now, for the $1 million question: What in the world does this have to do with caregiving? Well, I'll tell you, this is a situation I would describe to candidates interviewing for positions in my agency—I want to know how they would respond if they were in Joanne's shoes. This has nothing to do with caregiving because it could happen in any place where people are waiting in line. On the other hand, it has everything to do with caregiving because the person's response reveals something about their personal character. Do you want to hire someone who would respond in a confrontational manner and engage in a needless power struggle with a person who is behaving rudely?

In our training film, *The Caregiving Personality*, Roger MacNamara points out, "In a situation where two people are in a confrontation, the person who walks away is the superior person. They don't have to feel superior to the other person, but they are because they stopped the conflict from escalating into a possibly violent outcome."

In your relationship with your spouse or significant other, there are times when you face challenging confrontations. At the moment of heightened anger and frustration, simply saying to the other person, "Dear, perhaps we should take a break from this," can be a relationship saver. I'm not saying that you should avoid issues, but peaceful, reconcilable outcomes have a far better chance of lasting than those that become violent. Otherwise, one of you will blurt out that unthinkable comment that cuts so deep, it will take months to heal.

I say celebrate! Celebrate your decision to back away from a conflict. We can analyze the rude patron's motives, mental state, or emotional intelligence forever, but we will truly never know what the cumulative causes of her frustrations were. Perhaps she was having a bad day, perhaps her child just got in trouble, perhaps she just lost her job, perhaps she's just dispositionally wired that way, perhaps, perhaps, perhaps....

I told my wife that I was proud of her for backing off. It takes courage and self-confidence to do that especially when we've always been taught to stand up for ourselves. So what that my wife got out of the store five minutes later. Does it really matter?

- We have new experiences everyday that challenge us. How will you respond:
- When someone behind you at the grocery store continues to shove their shopping cart into your heels?
- When someone cuts you off in traffic?
- When you see a friend to whom you've lent money making frivolous purchases after he's promised to pay you back over a month ago?
- When you encounter the next irate customer/ patient/consumer/ parent?

To respond with poise takes practice. See yourself handling these situations with tact, poise, and grace. Then, celebrate by saying to yourself, "Wow, I'm good!"

Breakfast Woes—Could This Lead To Abuse?

Rose is a 68-year-old female who moves fairly independently in her personal wheelchair. She is unable to talk yet communicates with others through gestures, vocalizations, and facial expressions fairly well. She lives in a 32-bed ICF/MR facility that provides a home to 16 men and 16 women on the separate sides of the house. Everyone shares some common areas in the home, and Rose frequently recreates in these areas with others. Rose is also known to be quite persistent at times and asserts her wants frequently. She can do much for herself but requires assistance with bathing, some grooming, and toileting. She has a favorable relationship with the staff. In fact, many of the staff know how demanding she is, but most enjoy her company as she does theirs.

One morning at breakfast, Rose is finished setting her space at the table as other ladies begin to filter into the dining room from the bathrooms, bedrooms, and living room. Rose wants to eat at this moment (her favorite breakfast dish is cinnamon oatmeal). All the ingredients for her instant oatmeal are ready for her (i.e., oats, cinnamon, hot water, and milk). She has a program to put on her napkin (placed around her neck). Rose prefers the napkin to be around her neck as opposed to laying on her lap. She goes to Adrian, a staff member, and holds the napkin up to her then Rose gestures for Adrian to place it around her neck. Adrian, who is regularly assigned to Rose, refuses and asks Rose kindly to do it herself first (as Adrian knows Rose can do this). Rose grunts in her characteristic frustrated tone and repeats her request to Adrian who again kindly requests that Rose do it for herself. Rose grunts louder, lays the napkin on her neck, wheels herself to Gary, another staff member, and repeats the request to him. Gary, too, denies any assistance because he also knows that Rose can do this for herself. She grunts louder this time and raises her hand as if she is going to hit Gary but doesn't. It appears to be a "warning shot" to him. Instead of hitting Gary, she goes to Kim, a third staff member, with the same result. This episode lasts for about five minutes.

Finally, Bruce, a staff member who doesn't usually work in this home, comes in to help in the dining room. Rose pleasantly gestures

Thoughtful Caregiving

to Bruce to help her with her napkin, which he obliges. Rose, now happy, begins to eat and carries on with her day. Meanwhile, the staff members who were trying to have Rose perform the simple task for herself are now angry with Bruce because he undid everything they were trying to accomplish with Rose. It was part of a formal program for her which the staff are required to document progress three times a day. Bruce is sorry for his assumption of offering help to Rose, and he apologizes to the rest of the staff. Afterward, they all continue with the daily activities.

During this episode, no one raised their voice, and the breakfast was observed by a supervisor as part of an internal quality-assurance program.

At what point, does the caregiver's role of companion supersede their role as teacher? Is the staff wrong in following the program? If Rose can already perform the task, why is it a formal program?

While no injuries occurred, how is the agency accountable for the possible injuries or unwanted consequences of such power struggles?

It's Time to Go to Work

The Byron Home is a newly built facility complete with all the modern-day amenities, lavish decorations, personalized bedrooms and plenty of space for everyone living and working there to spread out comfortably. It has a big yard and a covered picnic area that is used occasionally for special events and activities. The staffing level includes 1 staff for every 4 residents. During staff breaks and lunches, the level drops to 1:8 or 1:5.3. There is a full-time QMRP (Qualified Mental Retardation Professional), a full-time supervisor, and a full-time nurse who also spends time in two other homes nearby. Many of the eight men and eight women living in the Byron Home are independent enough to do many of their self-help skills, but may require assistance from time to time.

Bob is a 50-year-old man who moved to the Byron Home a year

ago and has seemed to have adjusted pretty well from his previous home, a larger ICF/MR house in town. He has been diagnosed as having a schizoid personality disorder, which is well-documented in his case history. As far as his expressive communication skills are concerned, he can crudely mimic words when he tries to talk. He has "happy" vocalizations and "mad" vocalizations that are very clear when he expresses them. His receptive vocabulary is quite extensive, and he understands most direction to household, work and personal tasks and requests.

The weekday schedule is that after bathing and getting ready for the day, the men and women eat breakfast. Once everyone is finished eating and the dining room and kitchen are both cleaned, everyone goes to work. Some of the men and women work at a community workshop while the rest all work in a private workshop (Work Activities Center "WAC") within walking distance of the home. Some of the WAC staff will help walk with the men and women to and from Byron, and some of the Byron staff will stay at the WAC to help the men and women with their work activities.

Bob's behavior plan targets correcting his "non-compliance" behaviors. He has been reported to be violent when he is in a bad mood and refuses to comply with the routine. His interdisciplinary team has recognized that "structure" is extremely important to Bob.

One Thursday morning, Bob clearly wakes up and is in a bad mood, which occurs occasionally. He characteristically grunts and barks at staff. He doesn't want to take a bath, get dressed, or even come to breakfast. In fact, he walks around his bedroom naked and will occasionally make his way to the common hallway or bathroom while nude. The staff members ask Bob to please go to his room or the bathroom. He eventually does and gets dressed without showering and his unpleasant grunting continues. It isn't directed at anyone in particular – simply anyone who happens to be passing by.

Bob refuses breakfast very clearly despite attempts of staff to offer him anything he wants. During one of the attempts, he slaps

Thoughtful Caregiving

away a dish and spits in the staff member's face. Tony, this particular staff member, instantly turns red and is clearly offended by Bob's reaction to his offer, but he says nothing and steps back. As it's time for everyone to go to work, Bob continues his angry outburst. According to his behavior plan, a wheelchair with a seat belt may be used as a last resort to transport him to/from scheduled activities.

Once everyone has gone to work, Bob is the only one left in the Byron Home. The staff all know what is expected of them according to Bob's behavior plan, so they make one last attempt to sweet talk Bob into walking to work. That attempt also failed. Seeing the wheelchair only adds to Bob's anger. Essentially, it takes three staff to restrain Bob, place him in the wheelchair and walk him to work as he is restrained in this wheelchair (once he arrives at the WAC, he continues his rampage).

The staff members all follow up with the proper documentation. One of the staff assisting (Debbie) is scratched during the struggle of getting Bob into his wheelchair and needs medical attention, which the nurse provides. Two hours later, scratches and bruises appear on Bob's forearms. An Unusual Incident Report (UIR) is started by one of the WAC staff members. The nurse quickly examines Bob, who is still upset. The UIR investigator is also prompt on the scene and begins digging into the potential causes of the bruising. In his discovery of the documentation in the Byron Home "Behavior Book," he locates Tony's entry for Thursday morning, and the nurse's entry for use of a restraint. In questioning Tony, the investigator confirms the location of Tony's hands during the struggle, which are exactly the location of the bruising. Tony further explains that these techniques were outlined in the behavior plan (and points them out to the investigator).

Bob is not restrained nor does he harm anyone else at the WAC but continues his shouting, barking and yelling periodically. This causes other men and women also working at the WAC to become upset. Finally, by late afternoon, Bob settles down and signs "happy" to his WAC staff member who has been with him all day. It's now 3:30, one-half hour before leaving for home.

The investigator concluded that the bruising was sustained during Bob's behavior outburst. The staff members correctly followed the behavior plan, which is closely monitored by the I-Team and a "Restraint Committee." On the UIR document, there is a section for "preventive measures" of future instances, to which the QMRP wrote, "Will continue to implement and evaluate Bob's behavior plan. Will also continue to monitor progress under direction of the "Restraint Committee."

Satisfied with the explanation and follow-up promised by the QMRP, the UIR committee filed the completed UIR documentation packet in the facility binder. Bob is five-feet tall and weighs 130 pounds.

- Is the staff wrong in following the documented program?
- Is the staff to blame for any injuries that occurred?
- How is the organization accountable for the injuries or unwanted consequences of such a result?
- What preventive measures would be more prudent?

~~Chapter 4~~

One Day A Provider, the Next A Consumer

Humankind has not woven the web of life. We are but one thread within it. Whatever we do to the web, we do to ourselves. All things are bound together. All things connect.

—Chief Seattle, Suquamish leader, c. 1780–1866

Bertha's Story—Part 1

The latest statistics are that 9 out of 10 of us will eventually live in a nursing home or supported living structure. With this reality in mind, I revisited Roger MacNamara's article "One Day a Provider, The Next a Consumer," which was first published over 13 years ago. Before you begin reading this four-part story, I would like to warn you that it may stir your emotions, particularly if you've ever had a loved one in an organized caregiving setting. The point I want to make with this story is that care providers (facilities managers) seek competence in the caregivers who work at their facilities. Suddenly realizing that you are a consumer instead of a provider sheds a new light on our whole profession. See if you can empathize with Bertha.

After almost three decades of writing and reading evaluations and treatment reviews, Bertha was listening to her own diagnosis. The doctor's statements were like incoming missiles whose warheads contained massive loads of dread and depression.

"There's no immediate danger," he asserted, but his reassurance was short-lived. "Your illness is untreatable and progressive. It will cause systematic retrogression in your current life-style to what I must forewarn you will become captive existence."

Her captor was a rare, genetically transmitted, neurological disorder that had only recently become active, but slowly and inexorably began terminating the services of her brain to its body's vital functions. Her doctor emphasized that her cognitive powers would not be affected until the latter stages of the disease's progress.

Bertha thought, "Was this supposed to be good news? I won't feel like a vegetable, I'll just look like one." She never thought she would use such language to describe a human condition, and she had no obligation to euphemize about her own future. This was not about other people. She had just become a consumer.

The doctor's recitation was performed at a studied, professional cadence with occasional sympathetic advice and caveats. "Advice and Caveats," the phrase sounded like a Jane Austin novel. No matter, Bertha was not hearing the doctor clearly. There was a second voice within competing for her attention. The doctor was courteously providing information but the other speaker was asking questions that he couldn't answer.

"How long will you be able to work, walk, enjoy life, take care of yourself and live with your family?" That last query was thermonuclear. She suddenly realized that her questions would not have answers—only decisions, and as her disabilities worsened, more and more decisions would be made for her.

The doctor was now discussing research. She was thinking about the cost of her care, where it would be provided and by whom. All of the platitudes that she had written into policies and mission statements about dignity, individuality and respect now seemed as trite and meaningless as they undoubtedly did to her employees and consumers. These were words, and consumers do not feel in words.

"Was it true, in this highly competitive culture, that dignity, self-worth and respect had to be claimed and defended and were not automatic entitlements that could be granted, bestowed or extended

Thoughtful Caregiving

because you were a human being? What happens when your human attributes are systematically destroyed by something that is only visible under an electron microscope? Do you retain your worth to others, to society and to yourself as you slowly slip away?"

She was sitting with her doctor, who was now silent and studying her, but she was elsewhere thinking about her future condition and where she would be living between dependence and expiration and how she would tolerate a "captive existence." And whether she had the right or courage to consider a Plan B (the Kevorkian way). The doctor was more perceptive than she had credited him. He interrupted her as if he knew that she was having unhealthy thoughts. "What other thoughts can you have at a time of personal apocalypse?" she said. "You will have one or two unremarkable years that will be followed by compromises," the doctor said. "Don't diminish your current life by dwelling on the future; rather, concentrate on today."

Sound advice; sound academic, emotionally-detached, not-personally-involved, professionally-conceived advice, she thought to herself. She was already there, wherever there was, and she suddenly knew what it would look, sound and feel like to be a patient. She was indeed dwelling on what she would be leaving behind and what would replace it. She was leaving behind a future that was supposed to have followed years of decent living and hard work. The doctor interrupted Bertha once again, but this time to inform her that it was time for his next patient. She had used up her quota of his time, and she could not usurp another patient's appointment. Consumers have to share everything with other consumers—especially time.

It was four o'clock by the time she returned to her office. The staff had left for the day. Left for the day and the evening to their homes, their families and their other lives, she thought to herself. Consumers do not go home. Patients do not go home. She went to her office to be alone. She might as well get used to being alone. A consumer has visitors and providers—not family and friendships. She sat in her office. She was a director, not of an agency, but of one of its largest divisions. This had been a decision. She had opportunities for administrative appointments, but had politely declined them. She had wanted a service leadership role without the politics of the upper echelon. Instead of a doctorate, she had chosen a second masters in an entirely unrelated area—French Literature. It seemed to her that specialization was sometimes confining and that opening her intellect to unrelated studies was more broadening than a "terminal" degree. What she had discovered was that she may have studied human beings in a different language, but their life circumstances, triumphs and tragedies were no different from those she observed in her employees and consumers daily. She had been content with her educational and occupational choices and felt that she had benefited by them. Having risen in professional stature by study and an assiduous nature, not by self-promotion or grandiosity, today she felt anything but grand. She felt cheated.

Bertha did not long indulge her feelings of self-pity nor did she attempt stoic acceptance as in "what will be will be." She knew that there was a fine distinction between being philosophical about one's plight and surrendering to it utterly. She would not disclose her illness to her family until she was ready. She knew that their first response would be to smother her with worry and vows of support. If she allowed her family to begin treating her as a patient, she would have her first experience as a dependent person. Instead, with the help from a friend and a therapist, she redesigned her life-plan. It was predicated on three assumptions: first, she would retain her zest for life whatever it took for however long she could sustain it; second, she would actively cultivate an inner peace about her future; and third, she, not her husband or her children, and certainly not a health professional, would decide the course of her life based on reversed developmental milestones. She remembered the doctor referring to the adjustments that her illness would necessitate as compromises. A compromise is not surrender, but failure to adjust to her changing condition would be sheer folly. When safety became the paramount concern, she would need personal supervision and support. In turn, she would lose an increasing amount of privacy and dignity. She could stubbornly cling to privacy and dignity, but at an increasing risk of falls and hospitalizations for shattered bones and injured organs—not to mention the possibility of head trauma that could foreclose on her most treasured quality of life, her cerebral independence. Her future life-plan had to have "safety nets."

When she needed personal care and support, then she would turn to the health services establishment. She would define when family support would become sacrifice and drudgery for her husband and adult children. She knew, no matter how much they would protest, when you have to provide daily, onerous care for someone you love, the relationship loses its quality through the inequality of the burden. She preferred to have uplifting, loving visits from them rather than prolonged dependence on them. If they loved her the way she loved them, they would understand that to watch them sacrifice would be as painful for her as it would be for them to watch her steady decline. She had to be clear and specific that this was a selfish decision, one to protect her pride, and for the love if not the fabric of family life. Better it be fragmented than stultified by her disease. That would be one victory she would not allow the rogue gene to claim.

The genesis of human services is people in need of support. We attempt to define what they will need and how they will respond to what we provide them. Is this ever truly possible? Will they need and respond to surroundings and personal supports differently from our loved ones, or, to the point of this chapter, differently than we do when their reality becomes our reality? In our training seminars, we ask participants to create a list of their requirements for a place in their future, where they might be confined for a lengthy convalescence or for the last phase of their lives. They often list the following:
- Privacy
- Dignity
- Decent food
- Safety
- Competent staff

Competent staff, huh?

Bertha's Story—Part 2

Let's get back to Bertha's story. Thinking of her future, Bertha considered personal safety as primary to her more cerebral freedoms: independence, dignity, choice, privacy and individuality. What she failed to appreciate, what we all fail to appreciate when creating designs for living, was the impact of group living and the organizational nuances that pervade it. Automobile engineers may have to drive their mistakes, but human-services designers experience theirs obliquely and therefore by inference. Groups and organizations have subtle and pronounced effects on individual quality of life. Perhaps the more devastating insight that can only be understood by direct experience is the sense of powerlessness one feels when he or she enters an organized caregiving setting. This impuissance is felt by friends and relatives as well.

Bertha and her husband sold their house and moved into a planned retirement complex, although he continued to work and she consulted at her agency as long as her health allowed. There were three sequential living arrangements based on the residents' self-sufficiency and overall health stability: 1) Fully self-contained condominiums; 2) Apartments with support services (linen, central dining, home health care); and 3) Skilled nursing care in a medical center.

Two years passed quickly, and Bertha's neuro-muscular condition slowly, inexorably declined as her doctor had predicted. First her dexterity was affected and then her balance and directionality. She had not been ill and was as mentally acute as ever, but she had begun to have falling accidents. Her husband insisted that he would retire to be with her more hours of the day. She informed him that if he did, she would divorce him and move into the medical center and not include his name on her list of approved visitors. He was not to change his basic life-style to accommodate to her disease.

Bertha moved into a cramped single room. She needed a walker but otherwise she was able to replicate her previous life in miniature.

Thoughtful Caregiving

She had a bed, a corner table, dresser and a closet-sized bathroom. Her husband bought her a small color television, clock radio and a laptop computer with printer. These latter devices were surprise gifts that he presented to her one evening the week before she entered the center. His thoughtfulness and concern for her future state of mind, evoked tears of gratitude and impending separation. What began as a few sobs rapidly became a painful exchange of loss and regret. And then they talked about the future, hers and his.

Staff were cordial enough, though often rushed, and they genuinely seemed to enjoy the fact that Bertha, among the scores of confused or mute patients, was able to converse with them. Most admired her wit and intelligence, but a few individuals thought she was a snob. Bertha was anything but snobbish. She was well educated and polite, but hardly unconcerned about other people's feelings. The residents were predominately Alzheimer's and stroke patients, who wandered the hallways, became lost and often mistook the room they happened to be in as their own. They removed other patients' belongings and concealed these in places the staff well knew were "secret" hiding places. Bertha would find them sitting at her desk and using her bathroom. Rather than complain, she joked to staff about her roommates.

Meal times were most unsatisfactory. She was accustomed to dining privately. Group meals were public and messy. She asked to have her food in her room. A curt employee informed her that any policy exception would have to be approved by the Nursing Director. Her request for private dining in her room was denied for reasons of sanitation. Bertha was accustomed to receiving letters from friends and relatives and especially her children. She had become an avid correspondent in the apartment and letters arrived every few days, sometimes daily. At the medical center, however she received no mail for days and then a pile would appear on her table. She examined the posting dates and knew that her mail had been accumulating somewhere. She asked an employee whom she had befriended to ask about her mail. Her staff-friend avoided the subject, until one day Bertha asked her directly. "I asked and was told that there are ninety patients here and that it was unreasonable to expect 'special deliveries.'" There were ninety patients, but the number of letter-reading patients was a distinct minority.

At Christmas, the center was decorated. Santa Claus visited each room and wished the occupants Merry Christmas. He knocked on Bertha's door and was surprised to hear a voice say, "Welcome Uncle. I haven't seen you since I was eight." He asked her if she had any special requests, and after a few moments of genuine consideration, Bertha said, "Eight megs of RAM would be nice." Santa Claus left shaking his head thinking to himself, "Poor soul lives in another world."

Each afternoon, patients were gathered in the dining room for bingo, music or seated exercises. Bertha chose not to attend. She despised bingo, and her physical therapy was enough exercise and becoming more arduous and painful by the visit. One morning, the recreation therapist stopped by her room to have a chat. She was concerned about Bertha's lack of participation at bingo. "I do not like bingo. I have recreation in my own room. I correspond, make calls, check on my stocks, read and watch television. I am also writing short stories."

The therapist responded, "You shouldn't allow yourself to make your room your world."

"It is my world. And I have visitors."

"It's not healthy to sequester yourself in your room to the exclusion of other patients."

"I'm not excluded from other patients," Bertha retorted sarcastically. "They wander in here all the time, day and evening."

The recreation therapist fixed Bertha with a disapproving gaze, stood and said, "You are not being very cooperative," and walked out.

Bertha made one request of the employees. "Please do not

rearrange my room. I have organized it according to a plan for neatness, efficiency and accessibility." Despite her clear and direct request, someone would purposely move her belongings. She did not know who at first, but for amusement and to satisfy her curiosity, she began to chart employee attendance and room changes. At first there might be multiple correlations, but absences and holidays soon narrowed the field. There were two employees who deliberately moved her possessions. She did not know their motives, but she suspected that they resented the fact that she had a single room and used it as an office as well as for sleeping. It angered her at first, and she was poised to make an issue out of their disrespect and cruelty. However, in this agency, complaints were treated in one of three ways: they were ignored, rationalized, or staff were given sharp rebukes, usually by a circulated memo that each one was required to sign. She decided to ignore the room changes. In time, these ceased.

Bertha's husband was under firm orders not to be her advocate. "You are my husband. Please confine yourself to that role. I have learned that it is best to accept the good with the bad." He thought about what she had said for days before sitting down with the Director of Nurses. Bertha had said "the good with the bad." He could not accept bad, and felt they should not have to accept it in a modern medical center. He made an appointment with the Nursing Director and asked her to tell him what his wife might have meant by "the good with the bad."

"Mr. Franklin, patients adjust differently to life in a facility," she advised him. "Some expect the same amenities and personal care they might have enjoyed at home. We have too many difficult patients and too few employees to cater to each patient's caprice."

"My wife is hardly a capricious person," he suddenly found himself saying more loudly than he had intended.

"Please try to control yourself, Mr. Franklin," she said. "We know that this is a difficult time for you. Let me assure you that we are doing the very best we can to make your wife's stay here comfortable."

He stared at her without anger. He suddenly understood. His wife was a patient, and he was the relative of a patient. She had been designated and labeled as had he. Roiling the authority structure of the center would do little except to create resentment. If his wife could accept, he could accept, although he would awaken in his sleep hearing the words, "We will try to make your wife's stay as comfortable as possible." Did they really think of it as a stay, and what do they mean by comfortable? He wondered when the Director of Nurses used the word "we," whether she really understood that "we" means each and every employee with equal conscience, compassion, interest, vigor and competence. Do we?

We teach new employees the basics of supportive caregiving. What are these basics? How soon does the curriculum lead instructors into the technical and mechanical aspects of organized caregiving? We then begin to read and have employees recite policy, procedures, schedules and protocols when the real basics are given more casual treatment. Casual does not imply that there is a lack of emphasis on dignity, individuality, rights, choice and quality of life, but the specific application of these abstract dimensions of human existence are often left as values and philosophy, again to be read and recited and very often forgotten in the daily grind of churning out services. While emphasizing accountability, data, incident reports and objective reviews have we forgotten that caregiving is a personal art?

We must teach employees how to overcome their first emotional reaction to occupational pressure and to follow a learned strategy of emotionally responsible caregiving. Most employees will not tell us when they disagree. We must eliminate traditional caretaking practices by supplanting these with new behavior. To achieve this goal, we must elevate caretaking from enhanced parenting to a provider support discipline. Perhaps most important, we must stress, not in orientation only, but throughout caregivers' careers that they represent humanity to consumers.

An Organization Is Structure Not A Life Form

When the two employees moved Bertha's belongings, they were assaulting her humanity. Everything we do in human services is personal to the individuals we serve, each comment, omission and act either enhances consumers' humanity or subtracts from their quality of life. It is not a contract. It is not sympathy. The relationship between employee and consumer is central to both parties' health and well being. The two employees who playfully or cruelly manipulated objects in Bertha's room tampered with her life. They may have thought their little game was harmless. One day they may know how it felt to Bertha as she lay helpless in her bed.

Service organizations must feel the need to change, not because it is the language of the day or to comply with pressure exerted by external forces. It must be an internally driven felt need; one seeks to do better and is essential to the interests of consumers, employees and the future of the provider agency. Abuse Prevention Specialists' seminars, videos and manuals differ from the offerings of trendy traveling consultants. We recognize that it is vital for employees to perceive training as relevant and therefore directly applicable to their circumstances. If they do not, they will dismiss it. This is the reality of introducing change in settings where pragmatics, not philosophy, is the rule.

Bertha's Story—Part 3

If an intelligent, aware and composed individual finds it difficult to exercise personal influence in an organized caregiving setting, how can patients or consumers lacking these advantages hope to exercise a modicum of empowerment in them? This question should cause insomnia for managers and service authors. We know the dilemma stresses patients and relatives.

Service providers must regularly appraise consumers' quality of life. If we could be consumers one day, how will we cope with the rules, rigidity, schedules, vacant time and apathetic and negative personalities in health-service organizations? We know what the policy books prescribe and proscribe and that mission statements contain cultural idealism, but what of consumers' daily reality? What defines the quality of their lives? It's not the plan of care. It's not interdisciplinary or treatment team meetings (unless these are focused on what truly makes a difference in consumers' lives). What makes a real and lasting difference is the way they are treated individually on weekends and week nights, when they are calm and cooperative, and when they are surly and antagonistic.

Consumers' Quality Of Life—An Illustration

Someone, a supervisor or recreation therapist, has proposed a wonderful day for us. It promises novelty, a change in routine, new faces and places. The day begins, however, with a nudge and a series of commands. "Come on. Wake up. Get up, and go to the bathroom." I am irritated and resentful of this assault on one of only a few quiet, private moments in my life. I prefer to awaken slowly, to allow consciousness to embrace not collide with me. The commands "Come on. Wake up. Get up, and go to the bathroom," are a rude awakening, and I don't care what has been planned for the day. I would be thinking, "This place stinks! This is not a good beginning and someone is likely to ask before the day ends, 'Is there no pleasing him?'"

We described how Bertha had planned her life in an organized caregiving community for an optimal quality of life with the full realization that there would be compromises to her previous lifestyle. She would accept less privacy in favor of greater safety and medical support. She was prepared for intrusions and occasional indignities, but she did not anticipate the extent to which her personal preferences would be judged and criticized by her providers. Even as a human services professional, she had not recognized the extent to which organizations tend to attack individuality when it is expressed too boldly. There will be employees who will like you, others who will merely tolerate you, and a few who may actively dislike you.

Thoughtful Caregiving

Consumers Are Often Judged When They Should Be Understood

You enjoy company and like to have conversations with your caregivers. They may see you are affable and responsive or perceive that you have an excessive need for attention.

You may be reserved and less inclined to initiate social interaction. Your caregivers may see you are a private person who demands little from them or they may see you as self-absorbed, withdrawn or antisocial.

You are neat and take time to arrange your belongings. You like order, and, yes, you become irritated when your space is rearranged. Some observers may feel that you obviously have an obsessive-compulsive personality.

You are a "free spirit," spontaneous, inventive and given to experimentation. You lack impulse control and have not learned personal responsibility.

You are happier on some days more than others. You are not depressed, but depending on your night's sleep or a bout of constipation, you may or may not feel gay and frivolous. You suffer from a bipolar disorder.

You wish to be left alone. You do not care what the schedule calls for, or what your caregivers believe you should be doing. You want privacy, some insulation from aggravation. You may be perceived as uncooperative, unresponsive, ungrateful, and by implication selfish.

Organizations often lack the time or inclination to guess what a consumer is thinking. Why do we refer to them as consumers? It's because they consume time, energy, patience and understanding. It's their nature to need, want, demand, reject and above all, to complain. For employees, consumers produce the daily grind of providing care much like restaurant diners create dirty dishes. We see it on some, though certainly not all caregivers' faces and hear it in their tone of voice. What we see and hear is resentment. How can a care provider deliver quality care when he or she resents the person to whom he or she is required to provide good care?

Who among us has not seen and heard the human-services veteran's incantation, "I can't wait for retirement." Allow me to introduce you to Walking Dead Dan. He walks slowly, speaks slowly, reacts slowly and has the effervescence of an old unstopped bottle of Coke. We cannot all be Bubbly Bouncy Bonnie always "on" and sometimes unbearable. What does she have to be cheerful about? What if Dan crawls his way to retirement and immediately suffers a stroke and awakens in a nursing home where his first sight is an expressionless, middle-aged man walking sloth-like toward him carrying a food tray and a bed pan? He nods at his attendant and asks in very slurred speech, "Hey, what's with this place?" His care provider says, "Nothing. I'm just on my path to retirement."

We enumerate consumer needs to remind us how we should treat them. Such enumeration also reminds us and employees of the impossibility of the task. How is it possible to accord privacy, dignity, normality, opportunity, individuality and choice for even small consumer groups? Groups? One is not a group. Is two? Or is it three, four, five, six, seven, eight, nine, ten or more? Whatever it is, it is a number. Numbers are an anathema to individualizing the human experience in organized caregiving. What consumers need, what we all need now and in the future can be reduced to two essentials. These require no memorization only the resourcefulness to help us and consumers attain them:
- Zest for living
- Inner peace

What do we emphasize during hiring interviews, initial training, periodic lectures or imply in our informal exchanges with employees? Why do experienced employees refer to our exhortations as "philosophy" and have their private aphorisms for our myopia? You people write the poetry, but we work the reality. One reason is

Thoughtful Caregiving

that despite our attempts to inoculate employees with values boosters, they hear and see contradictions.
- Protect them
- Watch them
- Be prepared for them
- Document their behavior
- Keep order
- Maintain the schedules
- Keep the place clean

The daily grind and quality of life are contradictions. Get them to bed, get them up, feed them, bathe them, dress them and don't let them sit around with nothing to do. And don't even think the words Fisher-Price or Toys Are Them. Find something that is adult, dignifying and interesting for them. How? What? Give us some specific, helpful guidance.

We teach new employees CPR, the policy book, treatment strategies, work rules, human-services vocabulary and basic care procedures. Then veteran co-workers teach them what they have learned from experience. Co-workers represent a culture within an organization, and new employees quickly learn that you are either a member or a potential quisling. It is better to belong than to be ostracized. You do what you need to do to belong.

Gone are the platitudes of the past replaced with techno-language and cultural value concepts. Perhaps it's time to think back in order to move forward. Do we or can we teach sensibility? Do we recognize and praise it or interrupt actions and attitudes that violate it? Does each member of the agency feel a professional organization around them focused on halting insensibility in progress? Do we model caregiving decorum with consumers and employees? Do we supervise for excellence and manage for more satisfying outcomes for employees and consumers? Do we truly appreciate that the goal of quality of life has one conduit, which is through employees' good will, perceptiveness, confidence, patience, kindness, predictability, self-awareness, preparation and emotional generosity with consumers?

Management contributes to quality of life. Immediate providers determine the quality of life. How are these contributions defined and combined for the most optimistic, satisfying outcomes for all concerned?

Take four pieces of paper and write MANAGEMENT, SUPERVISION, SUPPORT SERVICES and DIRECT CARE on each one. Under each, list the direct contributions each makes to consumers' quality of life. Then compare/contrast the lists. It becomes quickly obvious who has the most direct impact on consumers' daily lives. Knowing this reality, ask what management, supervision and support services are doing to support these efforts, understanding, poise and occupational self-esteem of care providers. Ask several questions:
- Who halts contentious caregiving?
- Who observes resentment?
- Who tests the atmosphere for tension or brittleness?
- Who looks at consumers' lives and employees' work life and asks, "Must things be this way?"
- Why can't life be more eventful?
- How can drudgery be reduced in providing and receiving care?

Bertha's Story—Part 4

Bertha exchanged her personal life for the safety of medical supervision. She knew there would be compromises, but she believed that she would be treated with dignity and respect. Isn't that our expectation for the relationships between employees and consumers? There is a fundamental, oft-repeated caregiving principle:

"Treat the consumer or patient with due regard for his or her dignity and individuality."

In practice, the principle is sometimes forgotten, disregarded or displaced by competing priorities. For example, if it is the organization's priority to maintain the daily schedule employees may be singled out by supervisors for reprimands if it isn't. "You're off schedule. What have you been doing?" The employee, having been duly chastised, returns to the consumers with one thought: Move it! We've got a schedule to keep. What happens to the caregiving principle quoted above? What if the employee blames consumers for his or her difficulty? In this instance, they're responsible for the reprimand. They caused his or her embarrassment or insecurity. In a medical center, there are implicit priorities. It's a quasi-hospital setting with add-on programs (e.g., recreation). When the supervisor says "clean," employees clean. They find themselves attempting to reconcile idealism with reality, but reality is greatly more powerful than philosophy.

It's a they-we-they world and employees are the WE in the middle. It is from this position that they see and experience caregiving. We constantly chide or remind caregivers, "Try to understand how the consumer feels. Put yourself in his or her place." Employees wish to know who feels their frustrations and conflicts and who knows how they feel about their responsibilities from day-to-day, hour to hour.

How would the Director of Nurses react to the information that two of her employees had purposely manipulated Bertha's possessions to annoy her? "We have rules. We train staff in the rules, we use progressive discipline for infractions." First, however, she would require proof of the allegation. Second, after verification, she would impose severe discipline on the offending employees, dismissal if it could be sustained. The proof would have to be direct observation of the offense. Would Bertha's claim suffice? The employees' representative would undoubtedly question her cognition even though at this stage of her illness she was as rational as ever. Her evidence could be viewed as circumstantial despite her meticulous charting of employee attendance and moved possessions. Perhaps she had imagined that her belongings had been moved. The employees had no reason to move her possessions and no memory of doing so unless they had inadvertently changed their positions while dusting her room. So, the accused remain employees, angry and with an attitude. They had been subjected to humiliation and almost lost their jobs. There was no justification for management's treatment of them. Henceforth, they will be more careful. It's a THEY-we-THEY world. The incident is quickly forgotten, but the infection has started.

Managers and supervisors are confounded by the sudden revelation of abuse in what they thought were safe, wholesome settings. There may have been unexplained bruises or nothing as tangible as a contusion. There was nothing other than the usual gripes and complaints, and these are constants among small and large employee groups. To gripe is human.

The infection isn't rampant, but it spreads slowly, one person at a time, selectively and by sustained contact. The agent is hiding insidiously among the daily palaver. Where isn't there a home or unit with any of the following characteristics:
- Troublesome staff turnover?
- One or more highly challenging consumers?
- Staff grumbling about progressive ideas such as:
- Giving consumers choices.
- Following complex teaching/treatment strategies.
- Maintaining impartial, clear and timely documentation.
- Arranging community inclusion activities.

We hear Quality Assurance, Qualified MR Professionals, and other support-service leaders complain: "Why do we have to put up with employee resistance and negative attitudes? Why doesn't someone do something about problem employees?" Which ones? The two employees who taunted a patient in a medical center? One vocal, negative provider in a community residence? A small cluster of disenchanted staff members who are increasingly gaining influence over co-workers? When will this influence become intimidation and control? What now? No abuse has been reported. No one actually

Thoughtful Caregiving

sees employees ignoring programs or scheduled activities. How then does anyone know a "core element" is adversely affecting the quality of provider care, and just how serious is this influence? The support staff know because they feel it. They know it because they hear it. They know it because they see it even though it's not sufficiently overt to report. Do you believe that the two employees who purposely moved Bertha's possessions will allow themselves to be caught doing something wrong or be reported by a co-worker whom they know can't be trusted?

What do doctors emphasize when discussing serious illnesses? Early detection is crucial to successful treatment. The prime difficulty with detection is the symptoms can be subtle and sometimes follow insidious routes. They appear, disappear and reappear. They look or feel like symptoms of less-serious diseases, which is the nature of insidious agents.

Suddenly you discover the presence of a negative split among employees, and you're not certain in which direction to proceed. You are concerned. You do not like what you hear or sense, but what do you do? Employees have the right to be protected from invasive suspicions. They aren't supposed to become cynical about consumers' progress or behavior and therefore shouldn't be subjected to skeptical oversight of their intentions. They shouldn't be the subject of discussions between managers, supervisor, service coordinators and co-workers. You are not certain that if you persist or insist on discussing your concerns that you might eventually be perceived as the problem. If you feel powerless, imagine how an employee who works next to the infection feels. He or she knows there is a problem, but he or she either lacks proof or the courage to report what concerns him or her. There can be repercussions:

- You will find yourself friendless.
- You may not have help when you need it.
- You may be falsely accused of misconduct.
- You may be slandered.
- You may be threatened.

Believe it or not, this isn't a remake of On the Waterfront. This is human services, where people come for help or to help others. This isn't a New York dock side. It's a developmental center, a community residence, a medical center, a nursing home, or a mental-health facility. Managers are hired to create and maintain abuse-free caregiving environments, and supervisors are promoted to oversee employee-consumer relationships and to ensure that work rules are followed. Furthermore, supervisors oversee service designers to assess, discuss and write support and treatment strategies and reviews for consumers. It is also a place where attitudes can harden, where practices can become coarse and the caregiving spirit can wither. Who hears, sees, senses, and acts on the signs?

- Attitudes
- Word choice
- Behavior labeling and reactivity
- Practices
- Frustration
- Resentment
- Victimhood
- Unresolved conflicts
- Individual employee instability or intransigence
- Insincerity
- Disillusionment
- Drudgery
- Emotional fatigue

These can be compounded by: 1) Supervisory myopia or apathy; 2) Management unfocused on quality of care; 3) Organizational hypocrisy; 4) Vacillating or uncertain priorities, and; 5) Formal and informal levels of care.

If the contagion has begun at a supervisory level, it can be greatly more resistant to detection and early intervention. The frustration of people in your organization who have responsibility for consumer welfare and who sense infection is twofold: 1) They aren't certain what to do; 2) They realize that the negative element has no real competition for its effect on other employees. In time, it becomes a powerful, silent undercurrent, and there is no immediately available equal or greater force that can reverse its direction.

The second conclusion, however isn't correct. Events can force recognition of the problem:
- A consumer is seriously injured prompting a criminal investigation.
- A worried parent writes to 20/20.
- A guilt-stricken employee leaves then reports the circumstance to a legislator.
- One of the miscreants becomes so arrogant that he or she begins to discuss his or her exploits publicly.

These are no pleasant means of forcing our attention to a troubled setting. There are consequences that cannot be remedied: the trauma to consumers and their relatives and the effects on the organization. The historic origins of abuse remain the causes of tomorrow's nightmares, such as bad hires, unjustified retention, the failure to see, the failure to act, unchallenged negative attitudes and practices, vague evaluations, isolated employees and unresponsive organizations.

Human-service organizations must be ever vigilant. Yet, like a flashlight, it will need fresh batteries and occasionally a new bulb.

Matthew Starr

~~Chapter 5~~

The Impact of Emotions

You give but little when you give of your possessions. It is when you give of yourself that you truly give.

—Khalil Gibran, Lebanese-American author, 1883–1931

The Nurse and the Supervisor—Part 1

Noreen, a nurse is preparing the morning medications for the men and women at a 32-bed ICF home where she works. Noreen is not usually assigned to this building but knows the men and women to deliver medically related services to while maintaining the normal rhythm of the day for the people living and working there. During her medication pass, Jake, a staff member from the UIR committee, calls Noreen requesting urgent attention on a UIR that happened the day before. Jake needs the information quickly because he has a meeting with the state UIR committee within the hour. For reasons unrelated to this morning's situation, this was the soonest possible time Jake could request information from the nurse assigned to this building.

Just as Noreen has secured the medication cart and prepares to perform her follow-up work on Jake's urgent UIR request, Traci, the supervisor for the direct-care staff, informs Noreen of another UIR. One of the ladies living in the home, Jenny, was found with some small scratches to her right leg. Noreen begins to feel her stress build. She has to complete the paperwork for Jake, finish administering the

Thoughtful Caregiving

rest of the time-sensitive medications, and now make sure that Jenny is okay, which involves more paperwork, time, and diverted energy from her scheduled tasks.

Noreen goes to the area in the home where the UIR forms are kept as well as the "Status" forms (used in follow-up reporting on previous incidents) in order to take care of everything on her plate. Upon arriving at the box, no forms are there. Noreen knows that Traci is responsible for maintaining the stock of forms in the house. At this point, Noreen snaps at Traci and says, "I suppose you want me to take care of Jenny and get all the forms here in the house, too! I can't do it all!"

Traci, caught off-guard by Noreen's remark, quickly responds, "I'll go and get the forms. I didn't realize we were out."

Unmoved by Traci's offer, Noreen snaps back as she turns away from Traci and says, "Never mind! I'll do it myself," in a terse, sarcastic tone. Walking away from Traci, Noreen continues to verbalize her frustration, "You guys have a case load of 4 people each, and I have a case load of 32! No one understands that my job is important, too! I can't get anything done around here because there are too many things everyone else needs done. I don't have time to do my own work! I try to help out, but nothing is here when I need it!"

Traci is upset by the whole situation even after Noreen returns and completes all of the UIR follow-up work for Jake's meeting and for Jenny's recent injury. Traci and Noreen do not speak to each other the rest of the day, yet Traci is still upset about the situation. She eventually goes to Noreen's supervisor, Allison, and tells her how rude Noreen was to her. Furthermore, Traci felt wrongfully attacked even when she said that she would get the forms for Noreen.

Allison knows that she must deal with the situation because it is not the first time Noreen has lost her temper with the staff. Noreen's demeanor with the men and women who live at the home has been observed as consistently positive, however.

Matthew Starr

Questions for Discovery:
- How should Allison approach the situation?
- When was the critical moment for Noreen that made it seem impossible for her to maintain her self-control?
- What are the ramifications for Noreen's explosive verbalizations as they relate to Traci?
- While no patient abuse occurred in this situation and all of the men and women who live in the home were properly cared for during this particular challenging time, what are the long-term effects of Noreen's verbal attack on the direct care and support staff?
- What could Noreen have done to prevent her loss of control?
- What could Traci do to fix the situation?

Before reading a dialog between Allison and Noreen, what are your thoughts?

The Nurse and the Supervisor—Part 2

Allison, Noreen's supervisor, is fairly new to the supervision field. In fact, Allison used to work the floor along side Noreen just two-years ago, before her recent promotion as a nurse supervisor. While Allison can quite easily sympathize with Noreen for her angry outburst having experienced similar if not identical circumstances of dealing with simultaneous urgencies, Allison knows that Noreen needs to be aware of how her anger affects the caregiving tone in the homes she works. While Noreen may not realize it, her verbal attack on Traci could affect Traci's demeanor when she deals with her staff and/or the people they serve.

In a follow-up meeting, Allison talked to Noreen about the incident.

Allison (A): What happened yesterday morning?

Noreen (N): What do you mean?

Thoughtful Caregiving

A: I heard you yelled at one of the supervisors.

N: Who told you that?

A: It doesn't matter. I want to know from you what happened.

N: Why? Am I in trouble?

A: Noreen, I want you to tell me what happened yesterday. Someone came to me and told me that you were yelling and were clearly angry–and I want to know what happened.

N: Well, I guess I should have known that you'd be after me, too.

A: Noreen, Stop. Let's just go over what happened together, please.

N: Well, in the middle of giving meds, I get a call from Jake who needed a status change report completed right away. So, I stop my med pass and get things around for that. Just as I'm ready to get that started, Traci comes to me with a new UIR on Jenny. Of course, nobody knows what happened, and I'm supposed to fix that too. Fine. I'm not complaining even though I still have to give meds to 16 people in 30 minutes. So, I go to get the status change form and the UIR forms and they're not there. She's supposed to supply those and they are frequently empty. It isn't the first time that I've had to go pick up forms – that's not my job.

A: Okay, did you lose your temper with Traci?

N: Well, I probably yelled when I shouldn't have, but it pissed me off to have to cater to everyone else's job when I have a hard time getting my own work done.

A: Okay; did Traci offer to go get the forms?

N: I don't know, maybe. I guess I don't know what you want me to do.

A: I want you to understand that I need you to keep your temper under control.

N: Am I in trouble for this? I just don't think it's fair for everyone to expect me to drop everything I'm doing for them. No one seems to appreciate it anyway. The direct care staff have case loads of four, and I have a case load of 32 and a license to protect.

A: I know., Noreen. Do you realize that you are still angry over this? Do you realize what happened yesterday is still influencing your mood today?

N: Well, you brought it up. I was fine until you brought it up.

A: Stop, please. Noreen, if you had a case load of 100 people, I wouldn't care. What I do care about is that you monitor and control your emotions here, regardless of the case load. Noreen, we all have to remain calm in stressful situations, okay?

N: Okay. Am I going to get written up for this?

A: No, I'm not writing you up for anything. I want you to realize that your emotions will trigger emotions in others. At the same time, we have spoken before about your temper, so I'm going to expect you to improve in this area. Your mood is part of your performance.

N: I guess I don't know when it happens at the time.

A: Well, you are going to have to work at it. It's going to take practice. I want you to also know that you can call me to help you with that.

N: I'm not sure what you mean.

A: Alright, I want you to try something. Okay?

N: I guess.

A: Good. I want you to think back to yesterday and replay the events as they occurred beginning with your meds pass.

N: Okay.

A: Now as you're informed about Jenny's incident and that you needed to go to get the forms—then you saw that they weren't there. You can feel yourself getting angry but instead of exploding, you say to yourself "Stop... Why am I becoming angry? They are just forms." Suddenly, you are able to handle the situation with poise. Now, instead of yelling at Traci, think of how you could have handled the situation your own way, peacefully, respectfully. Okay?

N: Okay.

A: Good. This won't be the last challenge you'll have to face. You know that, right?

N: Yeah.

A: So I want you to remember to stop, step back and think whenever you feel angry. You can call me anytime you need to talk about it, okay?

N: Okay.

A: Oh, yeah. There's one more thing I think you should probably take care of.

N: What?

A: There's a relationship that's now damaged that I think would be good of you if you repaired the damage.

N: Yeah, okay.

A: Thanks.

The Nurse and the Supervisor—Part 3

Now, let's apply our analysis of Noreen, her co-workers, the men and women living in the home, and Alison, her supervisor. Let us know what you think.

Question: What was the critical moment for Noreen that made it impossible for her to maintain her composure?

Analysis: The first critical moment for Noreen came when she immediately felt anger at Jake's request that she drop everything she was doing to handle a status-change report. A second critical moment came when she realized that there were no forms in the box for her to use for the necessary follow-up work.

The moment Noreen feels anger is the moment for her to insert a critical pause in her thinking. Thoughts control our moods and our behavior. While this is a simple strategy, it is not an easy strategy when Noreen, or anyone else for that matter, is not used to controlling their emotions. It will take practice daily to master a sense of command over one's emotions.

Question: What are the ramifications of Noreen's explosive verbalizations as they relate to Traci?

Analysis: Traci is now gun-shy about asking Noreen for any assistance. She's also shaken a bit and even angry at Noreen for yelling at her. Hopefully, Traci is able to put the incident behind her and approach her supervisory duties with grace, poise, and a keen sense of professionalism. She had the rest of the day to supervise activities, assist with lunch, and handle administrative tasks. Traci's ability to manage her emotions after Noreen's scolding now becomes an issue.

By the same token, if it hadn't been the situation with Noreen, it could have likely been someone or something else that would have eventually tested Traci's temperament and supervisory skills. Perhaps it would have come later that day or even on another day. Challenges of human emotions are a reality of delivering services to people. Therefore, Traci needs to expect to be challenged and be able to manage those challenges with exceptional style.

Question: While no abuse occurred in this situation, what are the long-term effects of Noreen's verbal outburst if they are not addressed?

Analysis: Despite the fact that the men and women living in the home were not abused, the caregiving setting will become negatively infected and contaminated if Noreen does not learn to control her emotions. If other staff members respond in a combative or aggressive sense to Noreen's yelling or even her possible foul moods, the home could very easily escalate into an exchange of anger where someone will eventually get hurt. Power struggles between direct-care staff

Thoughtful Caregiving

and Noreen will result in a divided house and ultimately compromise the care of the resident men and women. Chiefly, staff will eventually stop reporting any notice of injury to the nurse because they do not wish to challenge Noreen's mood swings.

Question: What could Noreen do in order to prevent her emotions from getting out of control?

Analysis: First, Noreen needs to know her emotional triggers. In this case, the mounting, time-sensitive health-care duties that befell Noreen were all tasks carrying a sense of urgency and importance. Truly, anyone in direct-service delivery can feel the pressures of these instances. Noreen needs to stop her thought process and deliver her health-care services with poise and style. Thought stoppage is definitely a way to do this coupled with rational responsible thinking. Moreover, Noreen needs to be able to handle her emotions at the same time she is devising problem-solving strategies.

Question: What could Noreen's peers or other staff who work with her do to help the situation?

Analysis: Recognizing that Noreen is upset is the first step, but it's not enough. Noreen may not even be aware that she is exhibiting anger so obviously. Noreen's supervisor needs to know about the situation. It doesn't have to be a discipline issue, however. Getting help is always a much better solution than waiting until it's too late. Noreen's peers can get involved and it takes courage on their part. Talking through the day and the events that transpired after-the-fact can be quite therapeutic.

Timing may be prudent, too. Honesty will go a long way to show that you as a co-worker are concerned about Noreen. For example, "Noreen, you are losing your temper too quickly and easily, which is making us all tense. I'm afraid you're going to do or say something soon that you'll regret. Please, get help or let me know what I can do to help you. We're all worried about you."

If you think we've missed something here, please send us your own analysis.

~~Chapter 6~~

Code of Silence

Put more trust in nobility of character than in an oath.

—Solon, Greek statesman & poet, 638 BC–558 BC

A sober air filled the room as the staff members all walked into the meeting room at the end of the day. Everyone's head hung in unison like mourners in a funeral procession. But it was more than sadness and remorse that weighed heavily on the minds of these five caregivers. Fear, doubt and uncertainty silently screamed from everyone as they began to sit down at the table during the last moments of their day before leaving for home. The silence was as loud and nerve-racking as awaiting the news from an oncology exam.

Arlene, the newest member to the team, broke the ice, "What do you think is going to happen, now?"

"We probably haven't heard the last of it," replied Derek.

"It's been going on for months," said Arlene.

"Months?" said Derek. "Try years!"

"Why hasn't anyone done anything about it? Why did it take so long?" Arlene asked.

"He was just building and building and it was like he couldn't stop it anymore," said Justine. "This whole thing is just sad."

Daniel reluctantly expressed his remorse, "Well, I just feel bad for him because he just started getting back on his feet and all. You know, from the divorce. I mean I really feel bad for his kids."

The rest of the staff all concurred with Daniel's comment as they shook their heads and mumbled "yeah, me too."

Another period of silence overtook the conversation. Arlene broke the silence again. "So, what are they gonna do now? I mean, are we going to get in trouble, too?"

Justine, the veteran caregiver of 25 years and who was like the mother hen of the group said, "Well, you know they're gonna probably interview all of us. I'd imagine that we'll see everyone from corporate here for the next month around the clock." She added with a splash of sarcasm, "That'll be a lot of fun."

Derek was focused on his thoughts. "Why did it take them so long to finally catch him?" he said. "I mean, everyone saw it coming. How could you not see it?"

"We better get our story straight," said Justine, "or you know we all will be up 'shit creek.'"

"What do you mean?" asked Daniel. "I mean I never saw anything! I'm not gonna worry about it."

"Have you ever been questioned in an investigation before?" Justine asked.

"No," said Daniel.

"Well, I have," said Justine. "These guys know what they're doing, and if they find out that any of us knew about this or what Scott has been like lately, then we all could face some time off."

"But we didn't do anything!" Daniel persisted.

"That's right!" Derek added. "We didn't."

"Yeah, I mean it's management's job to supervise, not us!" said Daniel. "I don't get paid to enforce policy around here. That's not my job!"

"You think they give a crap about that?" said Justine. They're just gonna say that we signed a policy saying that we'd report anything if we saw or heard of it. They're not gonna care about that."

Daniel argued, "But I'm not a supervisor. The supervisors are supposed to handle these things, not us."

"Wait a minute," Arlene interrupted. "I could be in trouble for this, too? I mean, all of us could be?"

"I bet that's what they're gonna try to do," said Justine.

"But I don't want any trouble," Arlene said. "I need this job. I haven't been here as long as you guys, but I think I do what I'm supposed to do around here. I think we all do for the most part."

"That's what I'm saying, too," Daniel said. "I don't think it's fair that we get could get punished for Scott's mistake. He's the one who did this, not us."

"I've been here a long time," said Justine. "I've been through this before."

All eyes and ears were fixed on Justine. She sat looking defeated and injured. The other four listened intently because Justine possessed some expert knowledge having been through cases like this before. They were looking for guidance, expectation, instruction, anything to ease their minds.

"It gets worse every time," she added. "Every investigation gets worse, and there are more and more policies we have to know every time.

"Surveys are a real trip, too," Justine continued. "Surveyors come into the building and are watching you even more closely. They read all of the investigations even if the facility can prove anything or not. They read all of the reports then come over here and watch you constantly. It's like someone's waiting for you to break under pressure."

More silence.

"I'm getting so sick of this," Justine said. "It doesn't happen that often, but when it does happen, it doesn't get any easier."

Thoughtful Caregiving

All eyes sprung up from the floor when Justine said, "You were right, Daniel. We didn't do anything. We didn't do anything to stop it. We didn't do anything to see that he got help before he got walked out of the building."

After a few moments pause, Daniel tried arguing. "I still say it's the supervisor's job to handle these things."

"I don't think Scott cares about that right now," said Justine. "I mean if you were Scott, would you rather hear your friends tell you to get help, or would you rather be humiliated as you're walked off grounds by security, probably lose your job, and have your picture posted on the internet for the rest of your life? Which would you prefer?"

"Well," Daniel said, "I just don't think it's right that we have to pay for his mistake. I still blame management for all of this."

After an awkward moment, Derek, almost in a pleading fashion said to the group, "I don't know what's gonna happen next. But if any of you see me begin to 'lose it,' would you please tell me right away?"

"Yeah. Me, too?" Arlene added.

"Me too," Justine said. "I promise I will. We all should promise each other to do that. I mean we owe it to ourselves to look out for each other and at the very least for the people who live here."

Seconds seemed like hours as the group waited for the clock to strike 11 p.m. With each passing moment, each one silently wished they could just go home.

Does this scenario sound familiar? Direct support professionals are often caught in a tough spot whenever they see a co-worker lose his/her temper and make a bad decision. One bad decision can lead to a case of abuse and ruin careers, reputations, and respect for the caregiving profession in general.

What did you notice from the scene in the staff room? What themes resonate in your mind about what was going on? In case you hadn't guessed, Scott, one of the direct service professionals in the home, was walked off grounds having been caught abusing one of the people living in the home. After such a traumatic event, what were the staff members in the room concerned with?

Let's identify some conclusions from the dialog and prose offered in "Busted for Abuse." There are painful realities for direct support professionals or "caregivers" if you will. As we learned first, Scott was recently dismissed for abusing a person living in the home, but the setting could have just as easily been a work activity center, a recreation room, or somewhere in the community for that matter. Scott lost his temper and made a bad decision—a decision that will cost him his job and any future working in human services for the rest of his life.

Second, Scott's decision also put his co-workers in jeopardy, indicated by the fact that they all knew of his temper and personal circumstances of having recently divorced his wife. Now, they all face possible corrective action because they failed to report any signs of trouble leading up to the incident. They're solemn reaction to his dismissal proves the point that there are multiple victims in an abuse case.

Where was supervision before all of this happened? Daniel's question is valid, to a point. While it isn't clear from the excerpt whether or not Scott was a good staff member who worsened or if he was intentionally malicious, his bad decisions caught up with him. Supervisors can't be everywhere at all times, so there is an element of trust in organized caregiving. Perhaps the supervisor knew Scott's demeanor and could prove nothing on prior service delivery observations. Perhaps the supervisor looked the other way or was intimidated by Scott. Or perhaps the supervisor was simply no good at his job. Courageous supervision sets the tone in the caregiving scene. Weak or no supervision is a foundation for disaster.

Did you notice the "we" versus "they" language the group used in the scene? The "we" were the caregivers and "they" were management

Thoughtful Caregiving

(or supervision). Clearly, this is a house divided. Whenever you hear we-versus-they conversations, the service area, whether it is a home, workshop or program area, is riddled with conflict—conflict that needs to be resolved and quickly. Otherwise power struggles between direct support professionals and their supervisor(s), direct support professionals and management, supervisors and management, direct support professionals and the men and women receiving services (it goes on and on) will develop. Surely, if conflict is not resolved or avoided altogether, the home will crumble like a house of cards from the slightest waft of air.

Whose job is it to prevent abuse? Everyone who works for the caregiving agency. While agency leadership certainly has to take responsibility for what happened and what should happen in the future to prevent such occurrences, line-level staff must also exhibit courage to hold each other accountable to do what they know is right—protecting the people who they've been entrusted to support. This can be just as simple as someone in the group saying to Scott, "You know, Scott, you seem to get angry way too easily. I think you need help." Who knows if it would have turned out differently?

(Ah! Wait for it...) "You're not my boss." You anticipate that response because it's a peer telling you that she doesn't think you can handle yourself. Fast-forwarding to the outcome of this abuse case, if you were Scott, I'm sure that you'd have preferred if one of your co-workers had tried to help you instead of ignoring your pain or intolerance of the people you were supposed to serve.

Did you notice that no one mentioned the status of the person Scott harmed—the first victim in the situation? This is even more evidence of a house divided—little concern for the victim. How is that person supposed to live with any kind of inner peace? If that person could speak for herself, do you think she wishes that Scott's co-workers would have intervened long before today?

When it comes to breaking company policy, many of us are familiar with the custom of not "ratting out our friends." Known as the Code of Silence, it drives walls deeper and wider between agency management and service providers. However, Management isn't innocent in creating the Code of Silence because of its historical way of responding to abuse and neglect and lack of vigilance in preventing it from occurring in the first place. Known as the "Cuts and Bruises" approach to abuse prevention, we sometimes believe that the notion that Management's new ways to punish people for committing abuse and neglect are supposed to scare caregivers into refraining from abusive acts. Direct Support Professionals would rather have opportunities for finding help for one of their co-workers before that person gets in trouble.

Facility management is responsible for setting the tone in the caregiving setting and the direction of the mission, and it's the Direct Support Professional's responsibility to serve the mission. Preferably stopping someone from committing abuse or neglect and at the very least reporting it, takes both groups (Direct Support Professionals and Management) to work together to create harmony where work and play merge into a peaceful household.

~~Chapter 7~~

My Brother's Keeper

The greatest discovery of my generation is that a human being can alter his life by altering his attitudes of mind.

—William James, American Psychologist, 1842–1910

Lonnie was an 18-year-old kid who was on a first-name basis with the corrections department personnel and the juvenile rehabilitation staff in his home county. The last straw for his probation officer and the department of juvenile corrections involved Lonnie hooking up with some friends to try and steal money out of a safe from the sheltered workshop where they worked. The judge for juvenile cases took Lonnie's "mild mental retardation" diagnosis into consideration and probated him to my home, a 32-bed, intermediate care facility for people with mental retardation, instead of jail. Fortunately, His Honor realized that jail wasn't working for this young man.

Lonnie arrived on a Thursday afternoon toting a youthful cockiness accompanying his six-foot, 200-pound frame. Definitely an alpha male, he entered the home and strutted through the hallway as though he owned the place. Unfamiliar with someone so independent, some of my staff members resented his arrival. He had an intimidating personality which was sure to upset our comfortable patterns of doing things from the perspective of the men and women living in the home as well as support providers.

Lonnie's presence reset everyone's thinking in terms of how we needed to provide services to someone who had his own way of doing things. Lonnie's probated arrival, by the way, was to become common practice in our facility—sending people with dual diagnoses (psychiatric and intellectual) for either respite care or rehabilitation. We were accustomed to providing support to people with more severe intellectual and physical challenges. Lonnie forced us out of the box.

He did things quickly, loudly, and firstly. Knowing only one speed, "fast," Lonnie kept us hopping. Immediately, we knew that this guy needed structure. Idleness was one of the reasons he was in so much trouble with the law. If he had nothing to do, he would spend his time voraciously chain smoking cigarettes. Watching him smoke cigarettes revealed to me part of his personality. Within a minute, he would devour his cigarette and be on to his next. He ate his meals in similar fashion. After wolfing down his meal within five minutes, he would take his dishes to the sink and move on to something else. Dinner conversation with the rest of us wasn't part of his world – it never was. After lunch or supper, his usual preferred activity was listening to Metallica blaring through his bedroom walls. Thankfully, he agreed to use headphones.

Within one day at the sheltered workshop near his new home (more like within 10 minutes), Lonnie decided that he wasn't going to be stuck packaging widgets (an assembly contract with a regional retailer). He refused to do "boring, stupid work," as he put it. One of the work activities staff members took it upon herself to insist that he get back to work (big mistake). Lonnie never resorted to physical violence but lurched forward to within a few inches of the staff member's face. His articulation was unquestionable; his non-verbal messages were clear; and her response was astutely correct – to back away. Her retreat was motivated more by fear than by an emotionally responsible act. Regardless, she did the correct thing and did not push back even though he bruised her pride in front of those for whom she was an authority figure in the work area.

He returned home and we spent the next 2 hours talking. It was obvious that this young man knew nothing about enjoying life. His home life was sad enough, yet he remained a dedicated and loyal son,

Thoughtful Caregiving

brother, and uncle to his family. He spoke about all of his criminal escapades as if he was bragging to his buddy in the locker room. Most all of his stories were met with a run in with the police, handcuffs, profanities, and a return to court.

Gradually, he opened up about his family, mostly his father, who paved Lonnie's way in life. A familiar face to the legal system, Lonnie's dad was in and out of jail frequently. Constantly in need of his father's approval, Lonnie was on the same course of self-destruction.

I had suspected there was something more there in our conversation because Lonnie's dad was dead. Unresolved issues with parents can be haunting for anyone. Then, he hit me with what I believed to be the raw nerve of most of his troubles. When Lonnie was 10-years old and incarcerated in the juvenile detention center, his father was also housed in the jail across the courtyard from Lonnie. There was enough of a visual path that the two could see each other. One morning shortly after his 10th birthday, Lonnie walks over to his window as usual to wave good morning to his dad. Dad does not wave back. Rather than a good morning "Hello," Lonnie sees his father hanging in his cell. Guards are present, taking photos and eventually they take down the lifeless body. In the meantime, this 10-year-old kid sits traumatized by his hero's horrific death. He is told that it was a suicide, but Lonnie is convinced that the guards set up his dad to make it only appear as such. Lonnie never shed a tear, and his sorrow remained tucked deeply away eight-years later. His contempt for authority remained unwavering.

Watching him as he described this story to me explained much. My role with Lonnie was to serve as a companion and support system, so I did not push him to get through his grieving process although it was clear that he was still angry.

Lonnie's plan of care was much different from the 31 other people in this home. Able to perform all of his activities of daily living (i.e., bathing, toileting, dining, etc.), he was more interested in finding gainful employment, moving back to his home county, and being on his own as much as possible.

I asked him what his dreams were, to which he simply said, "I want a job in construction. I want to play in a basketball league in the winter and a softball league in the summer. And I want to go camping two weeks every year."

His certainty of direction was refreshing to me. I thought that Lonnie's circumstances in life had not detracted him away from his dream. Work, play and rest through these activities just sounded like a lot of fun. Having been in human services for 15 years by that time, a construction job had its appeal because you can always see your results—an outcome that is very difficult to see in the caregiving profession.

One of the roadblocks to developing Lonnie's dream into a plan came in the form of direct care staff unable to unlock their thinking patterns to support a guy like Lonnie. Also, he had some restrictions outlined by the court, so our options were limited.

"We can't do that," and "That's not the way we do things around here," were commonly spoken in meetings about Lonnie or during conversations with regard to his arrival. "He doesn't belong here!" was my favorite (I absolutely agreed with my staff on this point, but my reasons were different from theirs).

There was something about this kid on which I couldn't put my finger. His confident swagger and quick unfavorable reactions to our benign systems and schedules for the home put everyone on the defense. He wasn't afraid to question authority, which was how some of the staff members viewed themselves. Seeing my staff become speechless from his simple and challenging questions was sometimes satisfying, I must admit. Breaking staff from relying on the schedules was like demolishing a brick wall with a toothpick. Any training our facility attempted with staff regarding individualized schedules hadn't really been embraced until now. I liked Lonnie very much.

Construction jobs didn't come that easily where Lonnie was now living. Acceptance of someone with a label of MR/DD in the construction industry was rare. Packaging and assembly line work were out of the question for Lonnie. It was a local painter who was part of the maintenance staff who graciously volunteered to have Lonnie work with him performing maintenance. George's position had been expanded to include not only paining, but performing some electrical, carpentry, and general repair work activities at our agency. It seemed like a perfect arrangement. After explaining that this real-world experience would give him some background knowledge in the construction business, Lonnie agreed to do it. He would be on the company payroll at minimum wage.

Union leadership then got involved and began pressuring the agency leadership, who began pressuring George and me. "How could we allow this? It's not in George's job description to take care of Lonnie. That's why we have direct-care staff that get paid a lot more than a maintenance worker." The union leadership clamored. Behind the scenes when they privately met with George, I don't know what all the union members said to him. George would not tell me. However, he told them to back off. George said that it was a difficult thing to explain, but he wanted to try it out and that it would be nice to have someone to work with instead of working alone all the time.

George's courage was inspiring and the union conceded to his and Lonnie's wishes. Then some of the executive staff came after me. Liability! was the word for that week. "What if he tries to beat up George? What if Lonnie gets hurt on the job? What if he slows down our maintenance schedule?"

I remember saying to my boss, "What if you remember our mission and keep Lonnie in mind when you think about our work here?" It's one thing to be personally pushed around by someone in legitimate power, but I wasn't going to let this hypocrite "suit" trample Lonnie's dreams. Everything she said spoke volumes to the fact that she didn't want him there either. She, incidentally, was the only executive staff who never visited or spoke with Lonnie while he lived in one of the homes she oversaw. Ultimately, she stepped out of the way, for which I was grateful. Now, we could get down to the business of Lonnie's life.

He was a "man's man." He liked to do manly things, so we got him a manly job four-hours a day, five-days a week. What were we going to do with the rest of his time? Physical activity was perfect for an 18-year old, promising construction worker. So, after asking him what kind of physical activities he thought he might enjoy, he said that he wanted to start weight training.

"You mean to tell me you want him to get stronger? We'll never be able to control him if he has a behavior!" Several of my staff furiously cried in opposition to his desire. Their general response was a case in point. Control and behavior were the operative words. They were focusing on how to control his behavior, while I was seeking ways to help him grow and improve his life.

Since part of my prior experience was as a fitness specialist, I opted to serve as his weight-training partner. It was settled—three times each week we worked out together at a nearby gym on campus that offered a weight training multi-gym, treadmill and basketball court.

Our workouts included a muscle-toning routine for the first four to six weeks followed by a strength-training regimen for five weeks. Lonnie not only worked out on the exercise machines, but also had to be my spotter. He learned partnership, responsibility, and trust in the weight room during our grueling workouts. It was fun for both of us.

Lonnie was definitely getting stronger, and we began to see positive results in Lonnie's attitude, work ethic, and commitment to his health. Additionally, another gentleman, Troy, moved into the home under similar conditions as Lonnie's. The two became instant friends. Troy wanted nothing to do with the weight room, but the two spent a good portion of their time in the house together listening to music, playing cards, telling each other their dreams. It was nice to see the two become companions.

Lonnie's work performance was also noticeably improving.

Thoughtful Caregiving

George and Lonnie accomplished much together during the four hours of work they performed each day. Soon, Lonnie was given greater responsibilities and began handling mechanical repairs to household equipment; he was operating small machinery and making decisions. By working alongside George, he also developed his ability to work as part of a team. The two counted on each other.

George's acceptance and coaching of Lonnie proved to have a profound effect in Lonnie's life. One afternoon, Lonnie was upset because plans for a move to his home county fell through, which made him very angry. In fact, he threw a temper tantrum. His anger spilled out in the form of swearing and yelling profanities, but he never physically harmed anyone. The bad news arrived right before he was heading to work.

As he sat in my office angry at the whole situation, he directed his anger at me. I tried to reason with him and explain what happened and what we were going to do next. He was not going to listen to me, not right then. He left the house to go to work. George was his next sounding board. George had no clue what happened.

Lonnie tried to take out his anger at work, but George stopped Lonnie with a simple question, "What do you want?" Lonnie said, "To get out of here!" in a loud, terse voice tone. George calmly asked him, "How are you ever going to get what you want when you act the way you are right now?" Lonnie paused between tears and said nothing. George cleverly followed up and said, "Sometimes, I don't want to do things or wait for things. You just got to be a man, suck it up, and move on." Lonnie sniffed a couple more times, wiped his tears, and began to walk with George to the next work site. Neither of the two mentioned the situation again.

Developing natural supports in this institution where I worked wasn't something to which I was accustomed to seeing. George naturally became a support system for Lonnie, not only at work but through weekly church attendance. Lonnie expressed an interest in George's church activities, and George offered to take Lonnie with him. Each week, George and his wife picked up Lonnie to worship, discuss life, and have coffee or lunch afterward. This 18-year-old "juvenile delinquent" was thriving and embracing the world rather than resenting, which is where he was when he arrived at our home.

His workouts were yielding some pretty impressive results. His body was taking shape; he noticed his growing biceps, chest, shoulder and leg muscles. He was growing stronger and healthier. He slowed his smoking from two packs of cigarettes per day to one pack per day. He was helpful around the house, performed chores, did his own laundry and even cooked for other members of the home for special events. He and Troy even helped me build a campfire site in the woods next to the house. Saturday morning brunches prepared over a campfire became a favorite household activity for most everyone.

One of the things that struck me as most interesting was sitting around the campfire in silence with Troy and Lonnie sipping coffee before the sun came up. It was one of the most peaceful experiences I've shared with anyone in my life. The crackling of the firewood, the glow of the flame on our faces, and the feeling of connection with the earth and with each other overtook us through the solitude and collective quiet reflection. No words—just living. It was magical.

After six months in the gym, Lonnie and I varied our routine to keep progressing. Concluding our latest workout, both of us were exhausted. Lonnie very happily flexed his arm and noticed his bulging biceps. "Hey! I'm really strong!" He continued looking at himself in the mirror flexing different muscle groups. I had no idea what I was about to tell him would have the effect it did, but I said to him, "I'm very proud of you." As I pointed to his heart, I said, "Because you've grown this muscle the most."

He stopped, looked down then back at me. Tears began streaming from his eyes. He wrapped his arms around me as if I were his big brother. He wouldn't let go as he must have cried for at least five minutes. When he gathered himself and was able to talk, he admitted to me that he never heard anyone tell him they were proud of him. The mere thought of this 18-year-old kid never having been genuinely praised broke my heart.

On our way back from the gym, we didn't speak but I could tell he was thinking of something. Right before walking in the front door, he stopped and told me, "You know, I made a promise to my dad that I would get my diploma, so I think it's time I go back to school." I thought to myself, "This is a great job."

Without Delay...

Every first Saturday in December at my agency was the annual Holiday Luncheon for the families of the men and women living in our homes. Lonnie's family told him that they were coming. His mom, sister and her baby, his brother, and step dad were to arrive at 11:15 a.m. to join him for lunch in the auditorium. Lonnie was excited to say the least. Having not seen them in six months, he was anxious to show off his home, introduce them to his friends, and enjoy their company. The event started at 11:30 a.m.

Family members of other men and women living at the home arrived, visited shortly with some of the staff, and then headed to the luncheon venue. Lonnie parked himself in the front lobby ready for them. 11:00 a.m. passed; 11:15…11:30…11:45…still no family. Half-past noon came, and Lonnie was still waiting. Over at the luncheon, people began dispersing to other scheduled activities following the meal. Lonnie continued waiting for his family back at his home. For more than two hours, Lonnie stared out the front window turning his head toward any moving vehicle. His excitement gradually turned to disappointment once it was time for supper. It was now 5:00 p.m. and his family had not arrived. No phone call—not a word. He loosened his tie as he fought back tears. He wasn't hungry, so he sat in his room demanding to be left alone.

I stayed at the office that day long after I was supposed to go home fully expecting to console him. My staff weren't sure just how to proceed, and they were just as disappointed for him as well. I just returned to my office when I heard the front door open (it had a distinct sound having an automatic opener). It was his family. I welcomed them and said that I'd be right back. Immediately, I went to get Lonnie. He raced to his family and gave everyone a hug. Along with the staff, I let out a sigh of relief. He showed his family around and asked them why they didn't come over for lunch. His mom said that they all stopped to eat on the way and did some shopping.

They stayed about 30 minutes and left. I couldn't tell how much it meant to his family to share the time with Lonnie, but that short 30 minutes made a world of difference to him. He saved his money to buy them all Christmas gifts, which he gave to them. They joyfully accepted, but failed to reciprocate not only then, but throughout the rest of the Christmas season. I don't think Lonnie cared, and I never asked him about it. I think for him, it was the fact that he could give his family gifts. I believe for Lonnie that in return, all he would have appreciated was being told that they were proud of him. It never happened.

Lonnie found a new home in a county just west of his hometown. Most important to Lonnie, it was closer to his family than his home with us. Through the Individual Options Waiver program, Lonnie was able to move to a new home, work in a new job, and as he had promised, return to high school to get his diploma. This man was on a mission, and life was good.

Everything happened quickly once it all started to roll. After a week of finding the home and a couple of visits, Lonnie was in his new home and had two roommates instead of 31 as he did in the home my agency provided. The excitement was confounded by a tragic event, however. Daniel, one of the other men who lived in the room next to Lonnie had been suffering for years from several ailments. Daniel died the morning Lonnie was leaving.

Daniel and Lonnie weren't really friends, but they weren't adversaries either. Daniel kept to himself around the home.

Thoughtful Caregiving

Nonetheless, his death rattled Lonnie. Through all of the emotional progress and maturity we saw in Lonnie, Daniel's death triggered emotions that remained unresolved from his youth. He was boiling that morning and didn't even know it.

I arrived at work and had just heard the news. Daniel was a popular guy around our agency. His suffering for so long was hard for everyone to take. Paired with our remorse, the entire staff were thankful that Daniel was no longer suffering. Daniel was an interesting and caring man. The veteran staff members still miss him.

Lonnie came to my office and was clearly excited about moving. His face was red and his eyes were widened exposing his battered yet warm soul. His excitement was uncharacteristically unharnessed and filled the house with nervous energy. Moving is one of the most stressful life events but dealing with death continues to top the list. Lonnie continued to brew internally while he spoke with others. His voice was shaky as he talked with me about Daniel.

"Daniel died last night," he said.

"I know," I said. "I'm going to miss him."

"Me, too. He wasn't doing very good, was he?"

"No, he wasn't."

"Yeah."

Lonnie then yelled at me with such force and anger that took me by surprise. "My dad didn't hang himself! He was murdered by those guards!" His eyes full of raging tears bulged at me like a charging bull. His muscular body tensed and took the shape of a predatory animal while his breathing became rapid and shallow through his tightly clenched teeth.

"I never said anything about your dad, Lonnie." I said. Instantly his rage vanished. He returned to his usual temperament. There is still a lot of work to do, I thought to myself. However, that work would have to be done at his new home. After we finished talking, I made sure to make my notes in his progress chart and recounted the incident to his oncoming provider.

We made small talk about the baseball game on TV the prior night as we walked over to the administration building to sign some final paperwork and say good-bye to some of the honchos. We made the rounds together, and then in a meeting with the executive staff, everyone in the room shook his hand and wished him well. The CEO, Director of Nursing, Medical Director, VP of Operations, Public Relations Officer, and VP of Human Resources (the HR VP incidentally played one-on-one basketball with him a few times on Sundays) all genuinely were happy to see Lonnie achieve as much as he did. The last executive to congratulate Lonnie was the VP of Program Services, my boss, who gave me grief for him being a liability on the maintenance crew. "Good luck," she said to him as she shook his hand.

He replied, "Thanks! ...Who are you?"

I bit my tongue and turned away from fear of bursting out in hysterical laughter. Our own VP of Programs was the only executive who never introduced herself to him before that day. Later, I thought how unfortunate it was for her to never see this guy grow. The caregiving staff and other support professionals in her charge all worked hard with Lonnie and were proud of his achievements as well as their own work with him. She, however, lost out. What a shame.

Three months later, on a Saturday afternoon in an auditorium, I walked slightly down the aisle and snapped a photo of Lonnie as he was being handed his high school diploma. His mom, brother and sister were also in the audience. I took a few photos of Lonnie together with his family after the ceremony, and I overheard him say to his mother, "I kept my promise to dad." His mom hugged him and told him how proud she was of him and how proud his dad would be, too. True to his character, Lonnie just smiled and said, "I know."

About a year later, I visited with Lonnie. He and his roommates had moved again to another more spacious home in town. He was working in a grounds-keeping job as part of a work group during the day and playing in a softball league, twice a week in the evenings. He hit an RBI double and a single the night before I visited him. Our time was short but enjoyable nonetheless. We did take in a round or two at the neighboring batting cage (competing to see who can hit the most home runs).

It's nice when a plan comes together.

~~Chapter 8~~

A Call To Courage

Courage is being scared to death but saddling up anyway.

—John Wayne, American actor, 1907–1979

My First Abuse Case

One of the most courageous acts anyone in caregiving can do is to turn someone in for committing abuse. Direct Support Providers as well as Supervisors feel the pressure to honor the Code of Silence for fear of retaliation from their co-workers. Although it seems to be less of a Code and more of an expectation for Supervisors, since they are supposed to handle these instances well anyway.

Work groups can reach high levels of intimidation as they pressure the mole, rat, or nark. At times, the pressure seems insurmountable. The facility is supposed to promise and assure that anyone who reports abuse is protected from such intimidation and retribution from agency staff. However, those who have stepped forward know otherwise. All of a sudden, no one will talk to them, or when they do, it's in an inflammatory way. Anyone who has turned in a coworker or employee for abuse, finds themselves working in isolation in the aftermath. In some cases, the facility management wants nothing to do with them. They want nothing to do with knowing that something terrible is happening on their watch. They fear the unwanted pressure of having to deal with corporate headquarters, irate family members and members of the press, and not the least of

Thoughtful Caregiving

all the pain and suffering of the victim who experienced the abuse.

I vividly remember the first case of abuse I witnessed. Marcus was a middle-aged man with developmental disabilities. I was his Qualified Mental Retardation Professional (QMRP or "Q"). This was the second week in my new role at the agency. Marcus wouldn't get up from the floor at his work area but preferred to sit on the floor and rip pages out of magazines. I had just arrived in his room and was going to take him to a medical appointment.

After asking Marcus to get up, his work activities instructor, Gerry, positioned himself behind Marcus, grabbed him by the neck with one hand and forearm and by the armpit with his other hand. Quickly, Gerry yanked and lifted Marcus off the ground with his feet still folded under his legs. Marcus did not possess the ability to speak but could indicate his pleasure or displeasure with vocalizations. In this instance, Marcus was silent. Marcus dropped to the floor and tried to escape, but Gerry's grip prevented him from doing so. "I said get up, damn it!" Gerry yelled.

I immediately said "Stop" to Gerry, and I also said that he was blatantly abusing Marcus. In a frustrated glare and intransigent defiance, Gerry said, "Yeah? Then you deal with him," just as Marcus succumbed to the strain of being held by his neck and armpit in midair. Gerry turned his back to me. The two other support staff and 10 other men and women receiving services were in the room and witnessed everything. None of the service recipients in the room possessed the ability to offer statements or could serve as a witness. The two staff members stared at me.

I immediately took Marcus with me and reported the incident to my supervisor who quickly began the necessary procedure of reporting and investigating allegations of abuse. Gerald was quickly placed on paid administrative leave, and I had the nurse examine Marcus for any physical injuries. A small amount of bruising eventually turned up on his neck and armpit. Other than the bruising, Marcus seemed to be fine physically. Emotionally, it was more difficult to determine but he at least appeared to be his happy-go-lucky self according to intensive, focused observation in the ensuing days.

Fortunately for me, I had a supportive supervisor who spent a great deal of time making sure that I was okay as well. It was the day after that I felt the after effects of the adrenaline. I can't tell you how much her support, listening ear and courage meant to me. I felt that I had her protection and security even though it meant an inescapable assault of investigatory paperwork and political turmoil for her. Everyone who has the courage to report abuse should have my former boss or someone like her in their corner.

What happened to me in the following days woke me up to the reality of the Code of Silence in organized caregiving. Gerald had worked for the agency over 20 years and was usually mild-mannered and polite to everyone. Waneta, his assistant who was in the room, pulled me aside when I returned to the work area and asked me, "What do you think you're doing? Do you know you're ruining Gerry's career?"

Stunned by her callous disregard for personal accountability, I didn't know exactly what to say. She continued, "I guess what I'm saying is that I didn't see anything wrong that Gerry did. I know Aimee didn't either." Aimee was the other staff member in the room during the incident. "We think you're just barking up the wrong tree." Her message was clear, they were going to stand by Gerry in the forthcoming investigation. I was on my own.

I received similar threats from more of Gerry's colleagues, including finding road kill placed on the hood of my car before leaving for home one day that week then someone ran their keys along the side of my car. The most powerful displays of the Code of Silence were just that—being ignored but watched at the same time. This occurred two days after I reported Gerry for abuse. While no one was supposed to talk about the incident until the investigation was completed, the informal channels of communication in our agencies never stop. Naturally, everyone in the work area was talking about it behind closed doors and certainly just out of earshot of me.

I returned from a meeting in another building and began walking toward my office, which was across the hallway from the time clock in the work activities center. It was exactly 4:24 p.m., and the entire staff from all the work areas were lined up in the hallway getting ready to punch out at 4:30 p.m. Usually chatty and jovial, they all glared at me as I walked to my office. Silence. I remember looking back at them; I could hear my own footsteps echo down the long corridor of marbled hallways. I could hear them breathing. I could hear myself breathing. I could hear the click of the time clock reach 4:25 p.m. No one said a thing. Without missing a beat, I unlocked my office door, looked down and saw a note under my door. "F———ing NARK!" was all that was written on it.

I sighed. They heard me yet their silence continued, as if they were on a secret hazing mission. Purposely, I left my door open and began working on some paper work that was necessary for a deadline. I was so used to working in a noisy building that the silence was almost distracting. Eventually, I heard the beeping sounds from the time clock as each staff member punched out. Still no words spoken, just beeps, footsteps, and the door swinging. Off in the distance, I heard vehicles pull away.

The truth was I didn't care what they thought of my reporting Gerry. Wrong is wrong no matter if you are a hardened veteran or a fresh new staff right out of college. People even warned me of Gerry's psychological imbalance and that it wouldn't surprise them if he eventually came in to the building and "went postal." I still didn't care.

Gerry's investigation took months to complete. Given the nature of the charge, he had to report to a pre-disciplinary hearing. Minor offenses usually begin with a verbal reprimand, but alleged abuse was something criminal as well. If found guilty of abuse, Gerry could serve time in a correctional institution. I was the first witness and had to give a first-hand account of what happened. Waneta and Aimee were next.

I wasn't privy to the proceedings of the hearing other than the time during my testimony. Later I found out that Waneta's and Aimee's testimony did damage Gerry's case because they testified that they heard me say "stop abusing him," which gave credence to my testimony. After being found guilty on abuse charges, Gerry appealed the ruling. The facility and union agreed to mediation. His union representative presented enough of an argument to allow Gerry to return to work after serving a 20-day suspension along with the understanding that breaking policy again would result in instant removal and criminal charges.

Did the facility cave? I cannot honestly say. My supervisor told me that she was extremely disappointed in the outcome. Ironically, almost one-year later, my agency underwent dramatic restructuring and I became Gerry's supervisor as well as the supervisor for many of the people who gave me the silent treatment in the hallway two days after the incident. I wasn't sure just how things were going to work out, but I knew that I wasn't one to begin a crusade of justice for those who conspired against me. I was committed to our agency's mission and I expected them to be as committed. We did have a rough start but I believe it was more a result of the restructuring and newly assigned duties and systems the staff were expected to follow rather than repercussions from Gerry's incident with Marcus.

The restructuring was badly needed, and the staff mostly stepped up to the challenge. They knew I expected them to perform. They knew I was not afraid to hold them accountable for meeting the daily challenges and making good decisions. We had daily meetings, solved problems together, eventually engaged in dialog instead of debating with each other, and slowly chipped away at the wall that divided us—Gerry included.

From that experience I discovered that courage uplifts people, inspires people, and changes people. I felt courageous because my boss was first. It was an experience I will never forget. While things worked out for me, Gerry and the rest of the staff, Marcus' family wasn't so cheery. Even two years after the incident, I can remember Marcus' sister crying in my office. "My parents brought him here to be protected," she said. "It's still hard to imagine."

I think of Marcus from time to time and hope he's all right, enjoying life and living in a supportive, accepting home and work place. Hopefully, his sister and her family have found the courage to turn the page on this chapter and have found their own inner peace.

Whenever I'm faced with a challenging situation where I know I must not turn a blind eye, Marcus reminds me with his unconditional smile and glimmering eyes. "Courage," they remind me.

Thank you, Marcus.

~~Chapter 9~~

Why Are People Still Getting Hurt?

One's dignity may be assaulted, vandalized, or cruelly mocked, but cannot be taken unless it is surrendered.

—Michael J. Fox, Canadian-American actor & Activist, 1961–

Indicators of Abuse

In an age of stiff punishment for people who commit abuse, even through delivering person-centered services, and with tough background screening of caregivers, why are people still getting hurt? In every state, we have laws, policies and rules telling our staff what is right and wrong, and we tell our caregivers time after time, "Do not hit the men and women, or we will fire you," only to go on to our next case of abuse.

Abuse occurs in the caregiving scene and sometimes in the most desirable of homes with adequate staffing levels. How could this happen? We know what the leading indicators or causes of abuse are:

1. Power struggles between people receiving care and caregivers
2. Responding inappropriately to the men and women who rely on us for support
3. Behavior plans that invite confrontation and conflict
4. Lack of adequate supervision

We know what causes abuse; therefore, we can prevent it. Part of the problem is organizational. We say to our direct service providers, "Give the men and women choices; respect them," but there are undercurrents in organizing and supervising caregivers that conflict with our instructions about choice and respect. Often, direct service providers are evaluated on making sure that they keep things in order and follow schedules. As a result, caregivers are encouraged to be controlling agents in the lives of the people who rely on them for support. Also, between emergencies, we don't know what to do, so caregivers "wait, watch and pounce."

What are some other ways that abuse can be built into the organization?

Why Am I Always Filling Positions? A Note About Advertising in Human Services

What do your help wanted ads say about you? Agencies in the healthcare industry always seem to have a classified ad in the newspaper and on career websites everyday. Somewhere, there is a need for a caregiver, a person who is needed by others to help them survive in the world. But, we don't want our caregivers to help the men and women just survive, we want our service recipients to have fulfilling lives full of joy and zest for living.

Some providers seem to have a revolving door for new-hire employees. Just as soon as a group of new staff is hired and oriented, some or all of them quit, either openly telling us that this isn't what they signed up for, or they just don't bother showing up again.

Let's focus attention on the classified ads your agency has in your local newspapers. How would you describe the language in your ads? Do these jobs sound interesting? Are the mission and the values transparent either in a good or negative way? Who is responsible for writing the ad copy? Do these people have any marketing background? Here is the wording for two classified ads I recently found. It didn't take long searching to find them.

"Healthcare company has full-time & part-time positions available for Direct Care Staff. Experience with MRDD preferred. Call ###-5555 or fax resume to ###-####."

"MR/DD Provider seeking professional Team Members to assist individuals with disabilities. Applicants must be able to work a flexible schedule including nights/weekends. High School diploma, valid driver's license, and reliable transportation are required to apply. Call NAME at 800-ZZZ-ZZZZ. Applications can also be downloaded at companywebsite.org."

Some other ads have taken a different route and included any and all kinds of jargon and acronyms specific to human services and take up almost a full column of ad space. After reading a job posting from one of my former employers, I felt like I needed a PhD before I picked up the phone to make an inquiry.

First of all, do these ads sound like they are special jobs worthy of attracting the best and brightest caregivers? If not, then why would we expect valuable candidates to apply for the positions? If so, will candidates see these positions as opportunities for growth or as dead-end jobs?

Part of our problem in managed healthcare is that it is difficult to find the right people to provide quality services to the men and women who deserve them. While it delays getting the staff to fill vacant positions, wouldn't it be better to stop the cycle of hiring "warm bodies" who we know are likely to quit eventually or who have no desire to grow? I'm not suggesting that someone with a High School diploma or GED isn't a qualified candidate. Some of the best caregivers I know have no post-secondary education, are good companions to people and are loyal to their provider's mission and values. They are living, breathing examples of staff development.

While the strength of a job ad is a small part of our hiring problems, remember that you have one chance to make a favorable first impression. What kind of impression are you making on prospective candidates? Don't just fill positions on a table of organization—find caregiving partners. The men and women you serve will thank you for it.

Where Is Our Health Care System Going?

I was talking with a friend recently who was lamenting his employee turnover for his group of long-term care facilities. Getting nursing aides to stay had become a real problem for him, and his veteran staff were feeling the heat from the extra workload, not to mention less time off. His first thought was to blame the economy then concluded that people these days just don't want to work.

Yes, we spoke briefly about his ads, recruiting strategy, and his hiring systems. While he is doing some progressive things in these areas, he inherited an agency whose organizational drift continues to push back at his efforts of change.

His next concern was that over the next five years, several of his staff will retire, vacating over 30 percent of his workforce. This is a significant problem when you think of the experience these people bring to the caregiving setting. The "hidden agency" knowledge alone stifles the mind. Jim, my friend, shook his head and asked me why it's so difficult to get good help these days.

Serendipitously, I had just finished reading an excellent book on understanding market trends by Kenneth Gronbach entitled The Age Curve. Not to oversimplify the problem, there is a trend in the American workforce that we can't ignore. While there is a change in values we are seeing in the prime workforce age, there simply are less people in the age cohort, popularly labeled as "Generation X" (born 1965–1984), than there are of their predecessors, the Baby Boomers (born 1945–1964). In fact, there are 9 million less people in my GenX cohort than my parents' Boomers generation. According to Gronbach, for every 10 Baby Boomer retirees, there are only 9 GenXers to fill their spots in the United States. This has significant business staffing and development issues, and this human-resource deficit will put a strain on the healthcare industry from all angles.

More care recipients will consume services while fewer workers will contribute to the tax base, which will in turn result in having to do more with less once Boomers hit their mark in long-term care facilities (LTCFs) or similar arrangements... Jim was not happy.

In a way it's exciting, I told Jim, because the healthcare system as we know it is going to change. I believe this means some policy changes will be coming. I look for Title 42 (Public Health) of the Code of Federal Regulations to undergo a new wave of interpretive guidelines (at least once in the next 10 years), and Boomers will see to it. Baby Boomers will begin to receive LTC services. Can you imagine the changes coming? If my parents are any kind of representatives from that generation, they most certainly will not be told when to take their shower, what to wear, when and what to eat, or when to go to bed. As Gronbach points out, Boomers fought authority quite effectively once—remember the 1960s?—and their experience of creating social change will revolutionize our industry—literally from the inside-out.

GenXers, according to Gronbach, have never really had to worry about finding a job partly because there has been a surplus of jobs to be had. We're still good people! Don't hate us! We're working hard, received our college degree, and are trying to keep up with the times.

So, what's a possible answer we can conclude from this reality? We need to become proactive. We need to start recruiting potential healthcare professionals at younger and older ages. These are our expanding market segments. Some Boomers want to keep working. Their life expectancy is longer than their parents' was (refer to Gronbach's book for details). Generation Y (born 1985–2010) will outnumber the Boomer population and their values are characteristically even more humanistic than Boomers and GenXers. The first wave of GenY is 25-years old right now, and showing young people the promise, fulfillment and joy of the caregiving profession is a long-term approach that can only help transform our industry for the better.

Thoughtful Caregiving

Technology is changing at the speed of light. In this endless technological voyage, GenY kids are comfortable. They were born into it. Don't believe me? Look at their toy boxes. Ask your five-year-old granddaughter to show you how to text message or twitter. This generation has a love affair with new electronic toys, yet they do get the fact that people will always need people. It's part of our human condition—to serve others and to be served. Good caregiving is a beautiful thing to see, hear and feel. It's our way of connecting with each other that gives us a feeling like nothing else. If we let that chance slip by our young people, then we will have missed a tremendously ripe opportunity.

My friend Jim, a fellow GenXer, knows that we've got a marathon ahead of us. It's a difficult yet worthy road. In the short term, we need to focus our recruiting efforts on finding people with humanistic values who may offer years of experience or the promise of emotionally responsible care for people who need us for support. If that means that we refuse to hire inferior candidates for the time being, then that's another investment. The person you hire is charged with providing care to someone's mother, daughter, son, father, brother or sister. After the interview, are you convinced that your applicant can handle the job? Jim told me in his most heartfelt Generation X language, "Tough love sucks sometimes."

~~Chapter 10~~

Anti-Caregiving Terrorism

If you do not wish to be prone to anger, do not feed the habit; give it nothing which may tend to its increase.

—Epictetus, Greek Stoic philosopher, 55–135

When Caregiving Crosses Over To Terrorism

Being responsible for the oversight and ultimate accountability for contaminated caregiving settings is no picnic. As you're walking into a home or place of work, you quickly conclude that there is something not right. It's beyond the fact that the men and women who are supposed to receive services are sitting around unengaged. Perhaps some of the men and women are involved in an activity, but it is done with such rote that there is no meaning whatsoever tied to the task. You catch glimpses of staff giving glares to consumers. Your stomach churns because you hear another consumer off in the distance scream or yell. All around you the tension is so thick that it weighs heavy on your chest. Your senses are keenly tuned in because you know that all around you there's foreboding danger.

Some exposés have managed to capture and report events where we see consumers with expressionless faces and a lack of zest for living. There are also individuals who are clearly living in fear. As of last night, there were more than 900,000 links to abusive acts caught on camera and posted on YouTube.com. A sad fact about this number is that these are only the instances caught on camera.

Thoughtful Caregiving

Twelve-years ago, a case Roger shared entitled "Bleak House" (named after Charles Dickens' book), was one of those homes we hate to supervise, monitor or visit. It was overrun with organizational drift after torturous attitudes from highly influential staff who poisoned the minds of the other caregivers, thumbed their defiance in management's face, and taunted anyone who dared question their way of doing things.

On one episode of a popular TV show that covered the topic of abuse at developmental disabilities centers, a witness being interviewed said, "There are employees out there who are just plain mean. They beat the crap out of those residents." Let us retain the flavor of his language. There are people working in day care, mental health, nursing centers, veterans' hospitals and developmental disabilities settings who are just plain mean. They enjoy their power over consumers. They have been placed in charge, and to them, that means total domination. It does not even matter if the patients or consumers understand why they are being battered. If they do not move when they are told; if they break something, wander, undress, sneeze or whatever; if it is annoying, these anti-caregivers lash out with utter, calloused disregard for consumers' humanity.

Let's introduce a radical notion—human service employees as anti-caregiving terrorists. Terrorists justify any action they take, no matter who is hurt, no matter how innocent the victims may be. Their acts represent [to them] grand defiance. Their behavior is demonstration of the oppressed striking back at their cruel masters. For these abusers, it is not the consumers, it is management. It is any manager with a title, formal dress and big paycheck. Managers who shuffle paper and would not know how to ask a consumer to go the bathroom. Managers who visit, smile and talk to consumers as if they were angelic darlings. Managers who do not know what it feels like when you have to come to work when you feel bad and take care of spitting, kicking, swearing little darlings for eight hours only to learn that someone called in sick and you will have to work a few hours of overtime. Managers who say that they appreciate us but keep us in scheduled bondage at wages our friends at McDonalds make as they smile and eat another free burger. Managers who always whine, "It's the budget! It's the budget!" when we are asked to pay more for our share of the health insurance. It's the budget. It's always the budget, but somehow the budget always pays management salaries. Whenever managers need an excuse for anything, they say, "It's the budget," or "It's regulation." There's always an answer, but answers that never really explain why.

Do you want to know the questions management never answers and cannot answer with the budget and regulations? Where are they when consumers are driving us crazy with their demands, refusals and bizarre behavior? Where are they when we feel burned out? Where are they when the latest idiot gets promoted to supervisor, and everyone knows that he or she is now a supervisor because of agency politics and not merit? Where are they when a large, brutal co-worker decks a consumer and turns to us and says, "You did not see that, understand?" This is the person they hired who is always talking about his love of guns.

There may be readers shuddering after reading the last paragraph. Such accusations from front line caregivers hurt. Angry employees brandish criticism like an axe. [We can hear what you're saying] – "Don't they know we have problems, too? Life is not that great for us either." WAIT. Employees believe you get paid to know their problems and to do something about them. You may not hear these harsh, distorted diatribes, but their co-workers do—sometimes daily. You can despise and disregard employees who defame you, but these employees do more than gripe. The really bad ones spread terrorism.

There have been cases where embittered, warped employees have brutalized consumers to express hatred of their agencies. These felons have mistreated consumers as a despicable means of expressing their contempt for authority. The terrorist mentality is dedicated to furthering its cause against a power they have decided is unjust, oppressive or unresponsive. An act of terrorism is a tragic, cowardly, misguided attempt to intimidate authority by victimizing innocent persons, consumers and employees.

I introduced anti-caregiving terrorism as a radical notion, but it is not an unknown one. It begins with unchallenged anti-caregiving sentiments. Once this malevolence insinuates itself into the caregiving culture, it can control all that occurs to consumers. Once it has gained control, it can and will terrorize consumers and employees alike. It gains control by coercion and a continuous barrage of anti-caregiving, anti-management propaganda. This employee element becomes an under-ground, a counter-culture and inevitably a criminal conspiracy. We call it anti-caregiving terrorism. Its leaders do not believe in your authority. They do not believe in consumer rights. They do not agree with your philosophy or policy. Once they have seized control, there is little you can do about it except to wait for someone to report them. They may openly flaunt their impunity to your authority while exercising a power that virtually dictates what occurs at hours when you are at home sleeping, enjoying a movie or attending a conference. Innocent employees learn who has the real power, and it is not you. You cannot control these people, but these people control them.

Do not attack. Do not deny reality. The solutions are good care, vigilance and strategic analysis. Abuse and good care cannot coexist. The abusive impulse is a constant threat, but our approaches must not alienate us from the very persons on whom we most rely for good care. 18th century British politician Edmund Burke is often quoted as saying, "All that is necessary for evil to triumph is that good [people] do nothing."

Recruiting Caregivers

How well does your agency recruit caregivers? Are you constantly having to fill positions? Here's some practical advice from Roger MacNamara on recruiting for the long term in healthcare.

http://www.youtube.com/watch?v=JH8cMFBB_VQ

Matthew Starr

Leaders and Managers

Too often, people confuse leaders and managers and think that they are one in the same—not true. In fact the two are opposite in nature.

A leader is one who points direction, creates change from the past and challenges the status quo. Leaders are somewhat discontented with the way things are, so their visionary approach to life newly defines what our organization does and how we define ourselves, whatever our business may be.

Managers are concerned with keeping things running in an orderly fashion and like the status quo. If it weren't for consistency, nothing would ever get done in the manager's eyes. Managers like the status quo and do what they can to maintain smooth operations. Changing directions is contrary to the principle of management in this sense.

If leaders create change, why do we need managers? If managers assure a consistent approach to doing things, why do we need leaders? We need them both to adapt, survive and grow, and we need them all the time, everyday, every hour in our agencies. If we never question why we do what we do, then we rarely see opportunities for growth when they appear. On the other hand, if we are constantly changing, then we flounder and struggle from a sort of organizational psychosis.

Once the leader sets a new direction and we can all agree to move forward, then it's time for the managers to shine. Managers clarify roles, jobs and actions, and are accountable to the mission. This is the time when we need people to show up and just work. We need people to sink their teeth into our systems and be productive.

In organized healthcare, we see an accelerated form of leadership and management emerge in a short period of time to correct deficiencies in federal mandates from a poor department of health survey. Otherwise, we risk losing our license. Leaders need to quickly define the new direction, and managers need to execute that direction and get people to voluntarily assimilate into the new ways of doing things.

The managers to whom I'm referring certainly fall into the category of carrying legitimate power in the organization, but I'm also referring to managers in the broader sense of the term. Direct support professionals, nurses, volunteers, and others who provide direct support to men and women in our homes, nursing homes, hospitals, and day program areas, need to manage tasks and at times get those we serve to do things voluntarily as well. This becomes a dangerous predicament for some of us because of the tasks and expectations of scheduled outcomes the leaders have determined should happen may not be readily accepted into the minds and hearts of the people receiving direct services. However, after a bad survey, positive real change is generally a relief to those missing out on the services they need.

So, what do you do when you have to implement policies and procedures that are different from past practice? You have to be able to take direction, correction and coaching with poise. Also, you must, must, must keep the Caregiver's Oath in mind. Leaders must, must, must understand and respect this, too.

Through times of rampant change or through smooth sailing, emotionally responsible caregiving must be the basis for our approach to being a good provider. Good care and abuse cannot coexist. Our emotional health, supportive nature, and thoughtfulness see us through both good and troubled times.

Misplaced Employees

This is going to be a really juicy one—just a warning! Everyone's favorite staff member. Can't you just hear their bottomless sarcasm, sense their excessive nagging and detest their unending barrage of declamatory observations? These individuals, who take pleasure in reducing the caregiving culture to a mechanical exchange of commands and a cynical workplace of gamesmanship, must have the chance to improve, and we've got to be there to see that they get our genuine assistance. For as much as everyone in the caregiving scene who would love to see our Misplaced Employee go at any cost, we will forever be judged on how well we treat our least-favorite employee.

> "We frequently complain about misplaced employees, but complaining about them does nothing to improve the quality of life our consumers receive. We learn to live with them to our eventual regret."
>
> —Roger MacNamara

Let's first begin with some operational definitions of what we mean by Misplaced Employees:

- Misplaced employees (MEs) are people who entered human services out of desperation or to pay for their current expenses and move on. They did not, however, move on.
- MEs are unemployed/underemployed persons who reasoned that taking care of retarded people wouldn't be too taxing until something better came along.
- MEs can be persons who were attracted to human services from some sense of misguided calling within them.
- MEs are persons originally who may have had good intentions regarding their responsibilities, but no longer enjoy them and dread coming to work.
- MEs are not automatically abusers, but given their attitudes toward responsibilities, they may be influenced by abusers or give in to act out their abusive impulses. Misplaced does not mean incompetent or insubordinate—only undesirable. We are as much to blame for our MEs. Also, not all MEs were born equal.

Do you recognize one of these?

The Walking Dead—these MEs work long hours without fatigue or change in their demeanor. They don't affect you that much when you work as long as you don't watch them. Their slow, slow, slow pace is methodical and hypnotic.

Chronic Vocalizer—some of our MEs are constantly vocalizing about something. They have an uncanny knack to find negativity about everything and share it with everyone standing in front of them. If they were in charge, everything would be different; although, they rarely edify exactly what changes would be except in the most general terms.

Stale Garbage—others are souring like stale garbage. Their stench is offensive to other caregivers. They cannot nor want to see the point. They demean those who embrace the point, and they coerce impressionable others causing them to miss the point of what we do.

There are some MEs who we may just have to tolerate, others who can be retrieved from occupational self-destruction, and others who simply have to go. Everyone of these MEs must have the opportunity to correct themselves with sincere assistance and guidance despite whatever negative feelings we may have for them. As we said before, fairness is essential—otherwise MEs become martyrs and cause further alienation within the organizational culture. Besides, we hired them. We allowed their tenure to lengthen without substantive comment. We owe them.

How Can We Expect Misplaced Employees To Accept The Basic Premises Of The Work They Perform?

How can we expect Misplaced Employees (MEs) and those who they negatively influence to accept the basic premises of the work they perform?

Human services employment is unique in one regard—behavior that we would normally regard as offensive or a violation of our individual and personal rights can be daily occurrences at work. In another setting, we might feel justified in condemning the person for their actions or striking back at them. This is not so in human services. We are expected to understand not react to insults, rejection and lack of cooperation. Very often being passive in the face of aggression is counter to what we have learned at home and from society. We read newspapers and listen to political opinion regarding the reasons for social problems and hear, "People must be accountable for their actions," and "The reason we have so many problems in our society is the lack of real consequences for criminal behavior or chronic irresponsibility."

In orientation programs, employees are told the opposite: "You must not judge consumer behavior or feel that you can impose penalties for what you believe constitutes right and wrong. You are here to guide, teach, model, explain, counsel and support and not to control or punish consumers." If you lose your tempers in response to an insult or aggression, you will be dismissed and charged with a criminal offense.

We must behave differently at work than we might at home or in our neighborhoods. We must accept mistreatment that would otherwise cause us distress. Also, permitting individuals to be insulting or threatening may violate our acquired values and beliefs. Two sets of rules (one for consumers and another for strangers) is a frequent cause of resentment, and vocal employees often cite this discrepancy as unfair. These same individuals are quick to observe that there is fundamental contradiction in agency philosophy.

You've heard them say it. "If our mission is to assist consumers to be independent, productive members of society, how can we permit them to scream, swear, kick, hit, destroy property and ignore us while we are attempting to teach them how to be responsible citizens?" The answer we most often give is because (wait for it...) "Punishment is not allowed here."

"Why not?"

"Because it's policy, that's why."

This is no explanation. If it is policy not to impose the order of rules on persons who need to learn the codes of society in order to be accepted by society, how can we hope to succeed? There are better explanations than reciting policy.

Punishment is counter-aggression, and its use promotes force as a means of solving personal and social problems. We now know that adults who have been punished severely as children are likely to be abusive parents. Likewise abused consumers become more aggressive.

Punishment encourages avoidance behavior rather than an understanding of the values associated with responsible living. For example, we may exceed the speed limit each day until we see a police cruiser. We have learned to avoid fines, but have not acquired the value of adhering to posted speed limits as a means of saving lives.

Children who are controlled by physical discipline may not be prepared for verbal limits set for them in school and in society when they are free of parental manual control. There is a reason for the typical adolescent child-parent crisis. The teenager has become difficult or impossible to manage physically. They've outgrown physical control and can exert their wills without benefit of the respect parents had intended to teach them.

Consumers have historically been subjected to harsh punishment, and it did not help them. They were treated savagely in institutions and made worse by their experiences. They were:
- Drugged
- Beaten
- Placed in locked seclusion
- Tied to beds and chairs
- Deprived of food
- Forced to perform hard labor
- Had their heads shaved
- Forced to perform degrading acts
- Deprived of possessions
- Restricted from visitors
- Lived long distances from their homes
- Were given substandard medical and dental care
- Ate mass-produced food with little variety.

Consumers have suffered the most brutal punishments imaginable. It did not teach them self-control, but made them antagonistic toward employees. It did not work then. It does not work now. People learn from social experiences not from pain and deprivation. Learning is not something we inflict upon children, consumers, or those receiving elder care. Yelling, threatening and hitting are expressions of our frustration and our lack of impulse control when we become angry. Anger and caregiving are inherently contradictory in purpose and outcomes. These are history's lessons our employees must know.

Central to person-centered planning and supports is knowing each individual's temperament, learning style, social proclivities and need for activity and solitude.

Getting MEs to accept the basic premises of what constitutes good care, the employee performance review is part of the puzzle here. It's not the only tool, but without an employee performance review that reflects their contributions to or subtractions from consumer independence and adult adjustments, you cannot respond to MEs. Designing the performance appraisal as a system of instilling emotionally responsible caregiving values in employees will give you more leverage when it comes to confronting those who refuse to get the point.

Of course, this is an oversimplification of the solution to the problem and is not intended to be the end-all, be-all answer to the human-services challenges. Several factors come into play when we have to deal with the joys of misplaced employees. Our experience with agencies in the performance review system has revealed meaningless comments on generic forms signifying nothing regarding the true measurement of emotionally responsible caregiving skills. We heard it before several times from caregivers, "These 'evals' mean absolutely nothing to me. I know I'm going to get my raise and there's nothing you can do about it."

As stated earlier, we will be judged on how we treat our least favorite employee. They should be afforded the opportunity to self-correct along with our sincere offerings to help.

Writing Classified Ads for Employment

I'm often humored by classified ads that agency representatives write and post in newspapers across the country. No kidding, here is a real ad I read:

> Registered Nurse, (City). This is a graveyard position. Performs duties concerned with the care of the sick or injured, prevention of illness and promotion of good health in compliance with (STATE AGENCY NAME) directives. EEO....

Rather than write the entire ad in this post, I'll just tell you that it listed more of the responsibilities the agency expects of candidates. The choice of words "graveyard position" surprised me. In case you are unfamiliar with this expression, graveyard shift refers to the overnight working hours running from midnight to 8 a.m.—not an actual nurses' station located in the middle of a cemetery. Please pardon the pun, but it does lead me to believe that this is a dead-end job and will attract the undead at best.

Related directly to ad writing, I had finished reading the series of books *The Wizard of Ads* by Roy Williams, who reminds us of the three rules of writing classified ads for employment. Let's take a quick look at Williams' rules and see what we can do to apply his insight.

Rule 1—The ad should be about the employee, not the job. "Are you dependable? Can you make a difference in people's lives? Do you have lots of energy and like to work with people? Do people like to work with you? Are you able to maintain a cool head when other people make you angry? How good are you at motivating others to do things for themselves voluntarily? Are you able to take challenges in stride, get your hands dirty, think on your feet, and through it all enjoy life? Are you willing to work odd hours? Would you like to be able to grow in your job and help build a home for people who can't do it themselves? Are you willing to learn about medical, psychological, educational, and social disciplines? If so, you need to call us right now. We want to talk to you! (Phone)."

If you're perusing the classified ads, can you imagine yourself in this role or not? Will the people you want to attract to your agency say to themselves after reading your enlightened ad, "Dude, this is so me! Where's the phone?"

Rule 2—Questions are the answer. Can you resist the urge to answer a question that was written for you? Once agencies learn to ask for exactly what they want and raise the standard in the ad, they'll probably see a different level of candidate coming through the personnel door to apply.

Rule 3—You get what you pay for. Yes, it's true. The least expensive way is far from your best option when purchasing ad space. When you're after that "X-Factor," it would behoove you to spend a little more. Disjointed *adspeak* does nothing to reflect nobility in caregiving. You want knights who are devoted to a life of service to others not indentured servants who show up for work to trudge through their shift.

Now it's the moment of truth. What do you want in your employees? You know you want to answer that question, don't you?

Competence Is Not Enough

Suppose you are a new manager or a veteran administrator who must interview for or justify your position each year. Whether you are a neophyte or veteran, you must pass this test to keep your job. You must prepare yourself until you are certain that you are ready for your interview. You know the likely questions. You know the issues. You are informed on the political, social and economic realities of modern human services. You are ready.

Picture yourself sitting before the hiring authority, a board or committee, who will decide your future. You are confident, but not overly so. After the preliminaries, introductions and the like, the chair person addresses you: "We have read your employment history and academic credentials. You are an impressive candidate/incumbent. We have one question for you today. You will have thirty minutes to answer a single question after which we will ask you for clarifications, explanations and augmentation. Are you ready?" You are less ready than when you first entered the room. One question? But you nod indicating your readiness to respond, but "one question and thirty minutes to expound on it?" The Chair also nods, establishes eye contact with you and asks: "Do you have the will to manage?"

Service Delivery Management Fundamentals

I remember after my football team won a game, my teammates and I would celebrate, congratulate each other, and enjoy the moment. Life was good—victory is a sweet tasting thing. That feeling lasted about 24 hours until we watched the game film. As the team reveled in celebratory glow, in the coach's office, our coaching staff was breaking down the game film, finding our weaknesses and making notes on our performance. It wasn't just the scoreboard that told the story; it was how well we performed and the manner in which we conducted ourselves on the field that was being critically examined. I still remember sitting in the classroom Sunday nights after a Saturday game, watching the films as our coach paused the action and pointed out our mistakes as well as our successes. I learned a lot during that time despite loathing the cumbersome process of grading my own performance in front of the team. It was after victories, not defeats, that we had our toughest practice weeks. My coach notoriously promised us that he would be watching us constantly so we would not let down our guard or begin to cut corners. After a win, we knew that we better be hustling and working even harder than we did the week before—there was no time to rest on our laurels. The coach was there seeing to it, and seeing to it too that the assistant coaches pushed us and kept us focused on improving. "We want to get better each week, fellas," my coach would say. "We had a good victory, but we've got to keep getting better, smarter, and quicker." My coach was vigilant. Rarely did he yell at us either—rarely was it needed.

The analogies I can draw from playing college football for me to take into caregiving are endless. Being involved in professional and community acting in my life now, I can say the same thing about the performing arts. I like having a vigilant director because I know that I don't know all the answers. My director's experience and insights make me perform better and assure that the audiences (my consumers) are satisfied with their choice of recreational activity.

As managers, professionals and supervisors, we can see and document evidence of emotionally responsible caregiving when it is in use. Immediate providers constantly are strengthening and refining their skills. Self-discipline of immediate providers depends on the persistence, strength and cohesiveness of the service delivery management team. Professionals, supervisors and managers must be monitoring caregiving settings to see that these fundamentals are present. If the monitoring isn't targeting these crucial elements of emotionally responsible values, then we are allowing caregiving to slowly and most certainly diminish to mere caretaking. Service delivery management (SDM) cannot, must not even for a week abandon this primary directive because a week turns into two weeks, and two weeks becomes a month, and a month turns into a year. What are we talking about?

"I will ensure by all means that the men and women who depend on my diligence are receiving high quality care."

Just as soon as we compromise this principle, we have put consumers in danger. It's our responsibility to what occurs to them thereafter. Abuse is a personal offense, and it damages the victim's trust. How can we possibly jeopardize our men and women's trust in us? Walking away from our vigilance insults them and makes it personal.

What Should A Manager's Personnel File Contain?
(Used with permission from *The Foremost Solution to the Abuse Problem: The Will to Manage*, Roger MacNamara®)

If you were to look in a manager's personnel file, what should you find? The file should reflect their skill and vigor in pursuing high-quality care and protecting consumers from misplaced employees. Each member of the service delivery management crew should have periodic performance appraisals—THE central features of which contain:

- Provides continuous impetus for care by principles, not methods.
- Actively discourages behavior-reactive care.
- Maintains communication to all caregiving scenes.
- Monitors immediate providers' attitudes, language and practices.
- Maintains summaries of consumer outcomes for comparative purposes.
- Designs performance appraisals based on consumers' responses to immediate providers and immediate providers' responses to consumers.
- Enrolls questionable employees into "occupational rehab."
- Samples consumers' quality of care routinely.
- Actively discourages "programming" in favor of natural learning.
- Conducts at least quarterly examinations of the emotional heath of caregiving settings.

If you are the administrator or manager of a human services facility, and your annual performance appraisal is scheduled for the next week. You've been informed that the above 10 items are the performance criteria on which you are to be evaluated. Your ability to document such efforts to satisfy these service delivery management requirements will determine your future at the agency. Will you be ready?

Matthew Starr

Your Evaluation Is Biased!

Jenny burst into the office, pointed her finger at Glenn, and said, "I've got a bone to pick with you." Never mind that there were three other staff in the room who were engaged in their own meeting with Glenn. Jenny wasn't kidding. She got everyone's attention.

Despite his calm outward appearance, Jenny caught Glenn off-guard. He had to think momentarily before responding.

"Jenny, now isn't the time to get into this. I need to finish up here. Would you please wait?" said Glenn.

"You better come and get me right away because this is just wrong," Jenny demanded as she left the room slamming the door behind her. The three staff members stared uncomfortably at the floor until Jenny was gone. Slightly shaken, Glenn sighed and continued his meeting with the staff. Glenn is this group home's supervisor. He's the supervisor for three other group homes as well.

Evaluating employees can be one of the most reaffirming and uplifting duties a manager can provide for the agency and for the employee. The performance appraisal can also be one of the most anxiety-producing tasks for someone else. In organized caregiving, managers and supervisors have the task of assuring that each employee is serving the organization's mission, which is tied to providing opportunities for service recipients to enjoy life (or it ought to include something as such). Moreover, supervisors and managers are evaluated largely on how their employees perform. Similar to a basketball coach; the coach is evaluated based on his team's performance or record. Not to oversimplify the structure, but the players must understand and serve their program's mission. Otherwise, the coach sits them on the bench or removes them from the team.

Organized caregiving has had waves of personnel providing services and supervising front-line staff. Some supervisors may have been in their roles for years while others are newer, younger supervisors who have the task of combating organizational drift and a structural inertia that would test even the most patient coach.

Managers or supervisors who believe or need the assurance that they can be career administrators are victims of the attitude Roger MacNamara calls "the triumph of hope for experience." Agency leadership must critically examine whether or not their managers are good coaches or did they aspire to a legitimate power position because of seniority? Are they evaluating employees with the expectations of the mission? Are the care providers under their supervision growing personally and professionally?

Glenn is good at his job. He is considered a strong leader and a courageous manager because of his poise, loving rapport with the men and women who live in the homes he supervises, and he is willing to make unpopular decisions when they must be made. As such, his staff give him a great deal of respect. There are some exceptions—notably Jenny.

Glenn finishes his meeting, returns some phone messages, then seeks out Jenny. The two of them go to his office and she begins to speak her mind.

"What is this all about? You didn't rate me 'above' in any area on my 'eval!' Last year, I had 'above' in two areas."

"Last year, you had a different person who evaluated you. He's no longer here," said Glenn.

"Well, I think this is unfair! I don't deserve this!" Jenny insisted.

Glenn responded calmly, "Jenny, you received an average evaluation. There are three ratings—below, meets, and above expectations. In the above expectations rating, you must demonstrate that you go above and beyond the call of duty. Meets expectations covers a wide range of performance. Your evaluation reflects an average performance, not below."

"That's what I mean," said Jenny.

"Me, too."

Taken by surprise for a moment, Jenny thought about his last comment and said, "Well, it's just not fair!"

Glenn was ready. He had done his homework and took evaluations seriously. "Jenny, we discussed this before I completed your evaluation. Your performance does not reflect a high rating in 'Dealing with demanding situations,' and 'teamwork.' You lose your temper enough to negatively impact the rest of the team and cause problems when people are trying to solve problems."

"Well, this never was an issue before you came here!" Jenny said.

"OK," said Glenn.

"Well, I think you're biased. I think your evaluation of me is low because you don't like me," she claimed.

Glenn carefully explained, "There's something you need to know, Jenny. This isn't just my opinion. Other staff members, supervisors, and managers have noticed and commented on your quick temper and your uncooperativeness to help in certain situations. You follow through on your assigned duties without any difficulty, but you fail to give anyone any help when they need it."

Glenn continued, "This is nothing new either. We have talked about this before."

Seething, Jenny threatened, "Well, I'm going to appeal this, and you're going to have to answer to the union."

"That's fine," said Glenn. "It's your right to appeal, so we can take this up with the Personnel Director. But, understand that this isn't only my opinion of your performance. This is a collective opinion of several members of the agency who have noticed your attitude."

"Like who?" said Jenny.

"That's not important, and I wouldn't tell you if you guessed," said Glenn. "The point is that I expect you to handle these issues and make better decisions."

"Better decisions?" Jenny laughed. "I make fine decisions."

"Jenny," said Glenn, "just today you loudly and abruptly interrupted a meeting, slammed the door, and were loud and unprofessional."

Jenny's eyes began to tear up as Glenn continued to explain, "I expect you to be courteous, maintain your composure, and be respectful to others all the time. You may not slam doors, raise your voice or behave negatively even if you think you were wronged. These actions, by the way are a clear example of what I'm talking about in your performance evaluation."

Unable to find a counter point, Jenny reclaimed her position, "Well," she said in a calm voice, "I just think this is wrong." She left the room immediately. She did not slam the door.

Questions for Dialog:
- What qualities did Glenn demonstrate in Jenny's interruption to his meeting?
- What qualities did Glenn demonstrate during his private meeting with Jenny?
- How well did Glenn handle the situation?
- What could Glenn have done differently or better?
- What should happen next?

Maslow Won't Go Away!—Organizational Development for the Supervisor

Maslow's still got it! Just when I'm ready to move on to another theorist or trend in management, good ole' Abe sticks his head around the corner and says, "Yoo-hoo!"

Studying the prevention of abuse, neglect and exploitation of consumers brought me back to Abraham Maslow's Hierarchy of Needs. Assuming that you understand the basis of Maslow's theory on human motivation, I'm going to jump ahead to my point. If we really want to stop abuse from occurring, then we must hire and train emotionally responsible caregivers. Emotionally responsible caregivers are likely to have the higher order values—esteem needs and self-actualized needs.

When an employee is present in the workplace it's a means to an end (e.g., to earn a paycheck and/or to get healthcare for their families), which is not enough to assure good caregiving. When an individual's behavior is motivated by providing basic and safety needs to their family and nobody else, they—and we the service organization—cannot promise good healthcare for the men and women whom we are bonded to serve.

Belonging needs is the next rung up the ladder. Being one of the "guys" or "gals" is important because we feel that we are part of a group—part of something bigger than ourselves. It's nice to have people with whom we can share and be valued. Our lives are meant to be shared, so being recognized as one of the work group has value to us personally and professionally. However, what are you going to do when you see one of your group members hurt someone else? If you don't possess those higher-order value systems of esteem and self-actualization, then you cannot promise good care.

At the middle- and low-level order of values, the employee establishes no true occupational identity. The problem is that it isn't their fault. How is it not? This is the place where organizational development needs to mean something to the supervisor and front-line manager. Unless you've hired master caregivers, your staff may not know what caregiving excellence is. How would they know? Here's the way it's supposed to work. Give your staff genuine, real-time feedback on what is good caregiving and what is not. Feedback begets better decisions. Better decisions breed successful performance. Successful performance breeds genuine praise and individual recognition. Praise and recognition breed higher-order values. Higher-order values breed intolerance to abuse.

People who share in these values do not turn the other way when their peers do inappropriate and harmful things to others. Rather, they help them or turn them in to authorities. Staff members who would normally turn a blind eye to the truth need to be inspired and elevated, or be let go. It's upon the agency, with vigilance and courage, to see to it that employees have the opportunity to climb the needs pyramid.

Matthew Starr

~~Chapter 11~~

Which Way Forward?

There are two ways of spreading light—to be the candle or the mirror that reflects it.

—Edith Wharton, American author, 1862–1937

Is Person-Centered Planning A Deterrent to Abuse and Neglect?

Originally published in the Abuse Prevention Monitor® in December 2001, Roger MacNamara was making some observations of person-centered care philosophy that had begun to gain traction in service-delivery management at the time. Since then, states have invested a great deal of time and money in training staff in person-centered philosophy. I also found it interesting that Roger was talking and writing about person-centered care in his very first article in the Monitor® in 1995—before the wave of this service delivery method became common

Roger wrote then, "Person-centered care was not created for abuse prevention, but we have constantly reminded service providers 'good care drives out bad care.'" Examining his home state of Connecticut, he concluded that it has not had a clear and convincing effect on abuse and neglect prevention.

While we are currently examining data and hope to have a published study on the matter involving a review of the literature and the collection and analysis of empirical data, there are, however, some questions you can answer right now as you look through your

Thoughtful Caregiving

window to the caregiving world. Here are the questions Roger asked back in 2001. Moment of truth time:

1. Have you noticed changes at your agency since you adopted person-centered services, or is it the same old formula in use with new language and forms?
2. What differences exist between agency philosophy and daily care?
3. What frustrates staff the most?

Roger's thoughts from nine-years ago almost seem prophetic now. His ability to truly see the state of affairs in caregiving continues to weed out fads.

Applying humanistic theory to daily care is a universally accepted principle. In other words, no one is going to say, "No, we don't want to be humanistic to the men and women we serve." It is just as self-evident that care providers will never say, "We're not for abuse prevention."

But, now that person-centered planning and living have had some traction in human services, it's time to critically answer the questions "Are we succeeding?" and "How do we know?"

Empathy From History

Community versus institution has been a raging debate for decades, but too many antagonists do not understand why there should be a dispute, which is the reason that even today we have imperatives for one and defenses of the other.

There is not a living arrangement in existence that is not institutional in one respect or extent or another. One care provider can create an institution no matter how attractive the surroundings and a hundred of the world's best care providers cannot establish "normalized" living in warehouses. When we choose where and how the individual should live, he or she is automatically relegated.

How many children grow to adulthood unscarred emotionally from family, foster homes, school, and neighborhoods? We know more about life in the public institutions where reformers revealed their absolute and contrived horrors. Each care provider should know this history in detail in preparation for acquiring the proper empathy for their relationships with consumers. The purpose is not to shock them with horror stories, although surely these may emerge, but history teaches us much more than the nature of "man's inhumanity to man."

Lessons From History

Just as there have been ages of history, each era, Classical, Medieval, Renaissance, etc., building upon the successes and failures of its predecessors, so too caregiving has undergone succeeding waves of evolution and reform. The custodial era featured naked bodies, rivers of human waste, unfit food, contractures, day halls, dormitories, and wars of survival among the interred and between caretakers and the residents. Residents secured in walking restraints fell and suffered further brain damage. Seclusion and beatings by sadistic employees and "high-functioning enforcers" who were rewarded with cigarettes, coffee, and pseudo status, were not uncommon practices.

These were neither the artifacts nor the lessons of mass care. No matter how cruel the means, no matter how many injuries sustained or deaths resulted, the institution failed to control its captive population.

Residents in these institutions learned survival skills—retaliation, guerrilla warfare, and desensitization to pain, drugs, extortion, and intimidation. They survived and got their tormentors back by becoming more bizarre, aggressive, and self-injurious. They might wince, flinch, scream, and bolt, but their resilience was astonishing. They allowed themselves to be fed, bathed, and tied in bed even though they retained the potential for independence, though it could not be coaxed from them by educators and behavior shapers especially after the fruit loops, frosted flakes, and M&M "reinforcements" lost their novelty.

Performance-on-demand for the promise of a between meal snack was insulting. They refused to play this game to indulge interdisciplinary staff who had substituted procedures for learning and contrivances for true teaching.

Mandated and regulated care has failed as it, too, is an attempt to reduce learning to a series of static, repetitive steps rather than the dynamic activity it is and was meant to be. Required care was doomed because it was designed to satisfy regulations not people. Modern community care centers are as much driven by schedules as the sprawling institutions they replaced. Preferences become annoyances which are in direct contradiction to the tenets of person-centered care. There are two basic schedule formats:

1. Hurry up and wait or hurry up to be transported somewhere to do something of little value or interest to the person.
2. Immediate providers feel similarly about their jobs.

This circumstance could present a perfect opportunity for empathy between immediate care providers and consumers except the former are ordered to enforce compliance—always with a choice of course. Their lives are more dissimilar than not. Care providers know the truth of this absurdity, but must not risk insubordination. The consumers reject it because one more sanction is of little consequence to them.

Schedules are intended to create the illusion of a meaningful flow of activity and opportunities equally appealing to consumers and care providers. Schedules are management's means of controlling care providers. Outside officials do not immerse themselves in the lives of consumers or care providers and use schedule performance indicators to determine compliance with regulated care.

Person-centered care is a veneer instead of the essence of allowing consumers to lead us to desirable outcomes. Each time we write a goal or objective for consumers, we become the architects of their lives. Alternatively, each time we listen, observe and feel what consumers are attempting to communicate to us, we relinquish control and grant them the freedom to make their own lives.

Unfortunately, the almost overwhelming need to demonstrate service accountability has compelled providers to yield to external effects that may not necessarily reflect the best qualities sought by person centered life planning. In the end, the person's quality of life as he or she defines and experiences it is our ultimate accountability—not graphs, reports, meetings, scales, and assessments.

The fact of abuse in the caregiving setting means to us that person-centeredness has largely been unavailable to care providers. If their sense of purpose and nobility is lacking, then person-centeredness is automatically compromised by its primary instruments—consumers' natural or paid companions.

Malcolm had his own room. A visiting relative asked his care providers why he was in his room with the door closed. They answered he was sleeping. The relative entered his room and found him banging his fists against the bed rails and flailing around.

Another individual known for aspiration was given a peanut-butter sandwich for his lunch, which had been prepared and refrigerated the night before. By mealtime, the peanut butter was the consistency of firm clay, on which the individual choked to death. This was a death in the making. Investigators also found hard candy, stale French-fries and other debris strewn around the van used to transport this patient to his day program and on recreation events.

Person-centered care should focus the sensitivities of care providers on consumers' quality-of-life concerns, whereas previous approaches focused on "present problems" or how the consumer should change to be more socially acceptable and less an inconvenience to the caregiving organization. This unspoken mind set embeds the blame/punishment mentality, which is as evident today as it was in each era preceding. If you pointed out to care providers that their prime directive is to assist consumers to be comfortable in their surroundings, their responses will likely be skeptical.

The absence of conflict is essential to person-centered care and to the avoidance of escalating emotions from power struggles—the leading causes of violence between care providers and consumers. Respect for the feelings and sensibilities of consumers softens the care-providing environment and decreases calloused or indifferent treatment. Of course, this principle assumes that care providers will be accorded the same person-centeredness considerations that they are expected to extend to consumers.

If Not This Way, What Way Then?

For me the heart and soul of abuse and neglect prevention continues to be emotionally responsible caregiving.

The best way we know how to prevent abuse is to provide good quality care. Good caregiving and abuse cannot under any circumstance coexist. One case of abuse, neglect or exploitation wipes out the reputable provider's past and current ability to support people who need help.

Emotionally responsible caregiving remains the cornerstone of quality care. An irrefutable equation for effective abuse prevention includes emotionally responsible caregiving, and an unwavering determination by managers, professionals and supervisors to be vigilant to influence caregiving relationships and outcomes by direct personal involvement.

11 Preconditions for Emotionally Responsible Caregiving

There are eleven preconditions for emotionally responsible caregiving to be present. Roger MacNamara explains them in his caregiving manual, Not Knowingly Do Harm.

1. Employees are given explicit, written expectations that are reviewed with them frequently, formally and informally.
2. Managers, professionals, and supervisors will be firm, fair,

deliberate, and understanding with employees, but caregiving expectations will not be compromised.
3. The blame mentality will be resolutely discouraged.
4. Employee performance will be a shared management, professional, and supervisory responsibility.
5. Managers, professionals, and supervisors will recognize that the presence of two distinct cultures (i.e., direct caregivers and all others) creates an organizational rift, which can only be repaired with trust, support, courage, and conviction.
6. Undesirable employee behavior will be halted at once. If a manager, professional, or supervisor is reticent to approach an employee, his or her concerns must be shared with an administrative official.
7. Managers, professionals, and supervisors will actively influence employee attitudes and values and be evaluated on caregiving outcomes.
8. The quality of the work environment will be constantly monitored, appraised, and improved.
9. The use of professional jargon and trendy rhetoric will be avoided in favor of direct, honest, euphemistic-free language. Employee inclusion is predicated upon equality.
10. Managers, professionals, and supervisors will be specific, clear, frank, and persistent in monitoring and evaluating employee-consumer relationships.
11. Employees concerns for communication, competing priorities, stereotypical organizational roles, organizational hypocrisy, "paper" programs, and entrenched incompetence will all be addressed without lengthy delays. Employees will be given generous and genuine opportunities to pose solutions to problems that concern them.

Let me be clear. This is not intended to be a cookbook approach to the pursuit of quality care but a set of beliefs regarding the nature of human relationships. We presuppose that competent caregiving is based upon understanding, appreciating and respecting consumers' hopes, dreams, needs, fears and individuality. The employee's capacity to respond and assist consumers thoughtfully and not arbitrarily are regarded as absolute prerequisites for continued employment.

Stop, Step Back, and Think

When was the last time you were angry? What were the circumstances? Who or what triggered that emotion in you? Why did you lose your temper? How did you feel about yourself afterward?

None of us are immune from anger. It is an emotion within each of us. Yet, we each have our own emotional impulses or "hot buttons" that some people just know how to push. Anytime we come in contact with this person, it's like they have a tractor beam pulling us closer until they encroach on our emotional barriers, repeatedly striking our nerves. AHHHHHHH! I feel my blood pressure rising just thinking about it!

In *The Caregiving Personality®*, Roger MacNamara charts a course on how to deal with pressurized, blood-boiling situations, and it's good advice for anyone.* In MacNamara's Three-Step Process, he advises us to "Stop, Step Back, and Think." That's it. Simple? Yes. Easy? No. The beautiful thing about this straightforward technique is that it doesn't rely on a management fad, new company mission, or enlightened religious experience.

Here's how it works. When you feel tension growing inside you, when you feel anger rising to the surface, when you are ready to snap, say to yourself, "Stop" (known as the critical pause). In that pause, you've decided to take command of your emotions and to "Step Back." Now you've given yourself some time and space so you can "Think." Ask yourself, "Why am I becoming angry?" (Yes, you're supposed to answer yourself, too).

"Cooler heads prevail," is a notion that holds truth. When we think, we are using a different part of our brain than our emotions use, and we are able to generate options to deal with the pressures or the person getting under our skin (sometimes, they are one in the same, right?). Succumbing to anger severs us from reason. If you don't believe me, have someone videotape you the next time you are angry. Review the tape then try to convince yourself that you look good during the playback. Celebrities remind us of this truth when they are captured on film by paparazzi, which is then replayed on TV gossip shows and magazine programs. Having been pushed too far, these beautiful people (the celebrities, not the paparazzi) strike, spit, curse, and use hand gestures, which reminds us that anger isn't pretty, it's ugly.

MacNamara's "Stop, Step Back, and Think" technique is useful for supervisors and managers who insert themselves into situations where they must intervene and confront staff who are angry. While it wasn't one of my more favorite activities as a manager in a caregiving facility, I found this strategy to be quite effective. More than once, I had to stop employees who were engaged in power struggles with consumers. After stopping the emotional exchanges, my staff would inevitably attempt to throw the responsibility of dealing with the situation into my arms and ask the question that all supervisors and managers dread, "Well then, what do you want me to do?" And my answer (Wait for it...)? "I want you to calm down," or, "I want you to help this person calm down," or, "I want you to stop, step back, and think." My motivation for following this approach wasn't to dodge my supervisory responsibilities, rather I aimed to get staff members to change their thinking, to rewire their problem-solving circuitry, to provide real-time staff development, and of course, eliminate any likelihood of abuse. If I wanted to duck responsibility, I wouldn't have intervened in the first place.

Remember, we can control our emotions or our emotions will control us. Eleanor Roosevelt said it best, *"Anger* is one letter away from *danger."* If we are to eliminate the dangers in caregiving, we must also eliminate the anger and become more emotionally responsible caregivers. To do this, read, understand and follow *The Caregivers Oath* (see pp. 12–13), and encourage colleagues to as well.

Additional Reading & Resources

Balderian, N. (1991) "Sexual abuse of people with developmental disabilities." *Sexuality and Disability*, 9(4), 323-335.

Finkelhor, D. (1988) "A Comparison of the Responses of Preadolescents and Adolescents in a National Victimization Survey." *Journal of Interpersonal Violence*, 13(3): 362-382.

Finkelhor, D. & Browne, A. (1986) "Impact of child sexual abuse: a review of the research." *Psychological Bulletin*, 99, 66-77.

FinkelhorD. & Williams, "Children Exposed to Partner Violence" (with Janis Wolak). In J.L. Jasinski, L.M. Williams Eds., *Partner Violence: A Comprehensive Review of 20 Years of Research* (pgs. 73-112). Thousand Oaks, CA: Sage Publications.

Furey, E. (1994) "Sexual abuse of adults with mental retardation: Who and where." *Mental Retardation*, 32, 3, p. 173-180.

Furey, E. & Keharhan, M. (2000) "What Supervisors, Managers, and Executives Should Know About Abuse of People with Mental Retardation." *Developmental Disabilities Bulletin*, 28 (2).

Jacobson, A. & Richardson, B. (1987) "Assault experiences of 100 psychiatric inpatients: Evidence of the need for routine inquiry." *American Journal of Psychiatry*, 144, 908-913.

United States Department of Justice, Bureau of Justice Statistics. (2009) "Report on crime against persons with disabilities, 2007." NCJ 227814. Michael R. Rand and Ericka Harrell, Ph.D. http://bjs.ojp.usdoj.gov/content/pub/pdf/capd07.pdf

Keilty, J. & Connelly, G. (2001) "Making a statement: An exploratory study of barriers facing women with an intellectual disability when making a statement about sexual assault to police." *Disability & Society*, 16 (2), 273-291.

Holmes, Dr. William C. (2005) "Physical Abuse of Boys and Possible Associations with Poor Adult Outcomes." *Annals of*

Internal Medicine, Vol. 143, pp 581-586.

National Resource Center on Child Sexual Abuse (1992) http://www.prevent-abuse-now.com/stats.htm#Links

The National Research Council Panel to Review Risk and Prevalence of Elder Abuse and Neglect in Washington D.C. 2003 http://www.ncea.aoa.gov/NCEAroot/main_site/pdf/publication/FinalStatistics050331.pdf

National Center on Elder Abuse (NCEA) & Westat, Inc. (1998) *National Elder Abuse Incidence Study—Final Report.* Washington, D.C.: NCEA. http://aoa.gov/AoA_Programs/Elder_Rights/Elder_Abuse/docs/ABuseReport_Full.pdf

G. Allan Roeher Institute, (1995) *Harm's Way: The Many Faces of Violence and Abuse Against Persons With Disabilities.* North York, Ontario: G. Allan Roeher Institute.

Sobsey, D. (1988) "Sexual Offenses and Disabled Victims: Research and Practical Implications." *Visa Vis*, Vol. 6 No. 4.

Sobsey, D. (1994) *Violence and abuse in the lives of people with disabilities: The end of silent acceptance?* Baltimore, MD: Paul H. Brookes Publishing Co.

Sobsey, D. & Doe, T. (1991) "Patterns of sexual abuse and assault." *Sexuality and Disability*, 9 (3), 243-259.

Sobsey, D., Wells, D., Lucardie, R., & Mansell, S. Eds. (1995) *Violence and disability: An annotated bibliography.* Baltimore, MD: Paul H. Brookes.

Sullivan, P.M. & Knutson, J.F. (1994) *The relationship between child abuse and neglect and disabilities: Implications for research and practice.* Omaha, NE: Boys Town National Research Hospital.

Valenti-Hein, D. & Schwartz, L. (1995) *The sexual abuse interview for those with developmental disabilities.* Santa Barbara, CA: James Stanfield Company.